FROM BULLYING TO SEXUAL VIOLENCE

PROTECTING STUDENTS AND SCHOOLS THROUGH COMPLIANCE

Steve Cohen, Ed.D. and
Larry Altman, JD

authorHOUSE®

AuthorHouse™
1663 Liberty Drive
Bloomington, IN 47403
www.authorhouse.com
Phone: 1 (800) 839-8640

Published by AuthorHouse 12/15/2016

ISBN: 978-1-5246-5370-5 (sc)
ISBN: 978-1-5246-5369-9 (e)

Library of Congress Control Number: 2016920219

Print information available on the last page.

Any people depicted in stock imagery provided by Thinkstock are models,
and such images are being used for illustrative purposes only.
Certain stock imagery © Thinkstock.

This book is printed on acid-free paper.

Because of the dynamic nature of the Internet, any web addresses or links contained in
this book may have changed since publication and may no longer be valid. The views
expressed in this work are solely those of the author and do not necessarily reflect the
views of the publisher, and the publisher hereby disclaims any responsibility for them.

DEDICATION

To students who have been the victims of harassment
and to those who work so hard to prevent it.

TABLE OF CONTENTS

Appendix

Author Biographies

ACKNOWLEDGMENTS: STEVE COHEN

I would like to thank several people for their help in getting this book written and published. Special thanks to Marc Winkler, who is a great business partner and a great person. My coauthor, Larry Altman, is an incredible advocate for children and their safety at school. Max Garrison has yet again managed to do a great job of melding two authors with different writing styles into this book.

Additionally, I would like to thank the rest of the IntegraEd team. Andy Cohen for your amazing skills getting the computer to cooperate and perform magic. Dale Garrison for making the website and communication in general to work. Zoey Shopmaker and Macy Graham—you both are an inspiration to everyone for your strength, courage and communication skills. Lydia Young for your professionalism and gifts for understanding and helping others.

This book has been an amazing journey. The intention is to help school administrators, counselors, teachers and parents become more adept in their efforts to protect and guide students of all ages. The subject matter is very personal to me. There has been a suicide and a sexual assault in my family, and I know how deeply affected the victims and their families are by these travesties. This book is intended to get, and keep, the ball rolling on changing the paradigms in our society.

ACKNOWLEDGEMENTS: LARRY ALTMAN

There are many people that I want to thank for helping complete one of the items on my bucket list: publication of a book.

First, I want to thank my wife for always being there for me and never allowing me to give up on myself. Gail—you are my best friend, and if I have done anything good in the world, full credit goes you. I love you and thank you for everything.

Next, I want to thank the entire IntegraEd team who have honored me by allowing me to be part of this combined journey to help bullied students. This includes my coauthor, Steve Cohen, and teammate Marc Winkler, both of whom believed that I could do this. Steve's experience as an author has been invaluable. Marc has always encouraged my writing efforts and always supported me when I was bogged down in the midst of writing my portions of this book.

Another of my teammates whom I want to thank is IntegraEd's software genius, Andy Cohen. I don't know how he does it, but Andy is the teammate who develops the software that schools can use to help administrators and teachers prevent bullying and, as a by-product of that, keep our schools safe.

I also want to thank Dale Garrison, who is our publicist and keeps the world aware of what the team is doing to help keep students safe.

Thanks goes to our editor, Max Garrison. Over the past few months, she has had to put up with my off-the-beaten-path ideas and learned the hard way what Gail has had to put up with for almost forty-two years.

In addition, I want to thank my hero, and the hero of every disabled child and parents of disabled children, The Honorable Judge of the Missouri Supreme Court, Richard B. Teitelman. The encouragement over the years that he has given to Gail and me is beyond comprehension.

Finally, thank you to the heroes, school administrators and school staffs who dedicate themselves to prevent bullying in the school setting, helping the victims heal, as well as helping the perpetrators learn to stop.

INTRODUCTION

We, the authors, wrote "From Bullying to Sexual Violence: Protecting Students and Schools Through Compliance" because we are passionate about kids and schools. We care about student safety and wellbeing. We also care about schools and their ability to provide the best possible environment given their resources, as well as their limitations. And, we don't want schools to spend time and money with their lawyers. Our ultimate goal is to see schools take real steps to eliminate bullying, prevent suicide and reduce incidents of sexual violence.

Schools have students who are misunderstood. Schools have students who are at risk, and schools have students who will victimize other students. Know that, for a very long time, Title IX was not about this. It was basically about girls' and women's sports. That all changed on April 29, 2014. On that date, President Obama held a press conference where he signed an Executive Order expanding Title IX and started the ball rolling that holds every school district superintendent, every community college president and every university chancellor accountable to reduce and ultimately eliminate sexual harassment, sexual violence and sexual battery in their setting.

We know that businesses are very much Darwinian—only the strong survive. This should not be the case in schools, which are so different from businesses. Schools should be a microcosm of an evolved society, where the weak are held with the same esteem as the strong. The reality is that we are not there yet, but if the weak cannot yet be appreciated the same way the strong are appreciated, at least they ought to be protected. You will hear this theme repeated throughout this book.

We know that Title IX, in many ways, has been modeled after Title VII. Title VII is part of the Civil Rights Act that prohibits discrimination (sexual harassment) of a sexual nature from occurring in the business setting. The Supreme Court has ruled that the business owner is responsible to structure the business setting such that it is a "safe zone" for employees to be free from sexual harassment, and if they don't do the prevention, they are very easy to sue. If they do the prevention, they enjoy protections from legal action taken against them. The government, through the Department of Labor, has mandated that businesses take tangible and comprehensive steps to prevent sexual harassment from occurring at work. Additionally, if it does occur (despite the best efforts of business owners and operators to prevent it), then the business owner/operator is obligated to take steps to see that it does not continue.

Title IX holds the school administrator accountable to prevent sexual violence against students from occurring. Once the administrator has completed the prevention aspects of Title IX, the school's legal liability is limited. Just like Title VII, we find that under Title IX, if the school takes the necessary and required prevention steps, they will be protected in civil litigation and from consequences from OCR (Office of Civil Rights within the Department of Education). But, if they don't take the required prevention steps, they will be easy to beat in a legal contest. Let's say that the administrator has taken the required steps for prevention. When—not if—sexual harassment or sexual violence does occur, then the administrator now has new liability. He/she is now obligated to take steps to see that the perpetrator does not continue to discriminate against the victim and to see that the necessary steps are taken to ensure that the discrimination is not repeated, and others are not victimized. This applies to other forms of harassment as well.

The goals to eliminate bullying, prevent suicide and eliminate sexual violence appear laudable, correct? These goals seem like they should be fundamental to the process of education, right? Clearly, they should be. Sadly, however, many school administrators are unaware of their obligations under Title IX. *At this time, fewer than 1% of all schools nationwide are compliant with Title IX regulations.* There are laws that make it a crime to ignore bullying in 19 separate states. We know plenty of lawyers who act as counselors to schools whose position it is to let the schools get into Title IX trouble, so they can rack up billable hours defending the schools. That, in itself, is a "crime" with multiple victims. Compliance with Title IX helps protect students and schools both.

Our purpose is to let the school administrator, the school board member, the parents of students and anyone else who is interested know the obligations of Title IX and the state laws prohibiting an underreaction to these forms of discrimination. The first section of the book provides an overview of the laws and rules, some background information and a readiness test. In section two, you will find three detailed hypothetical examples of Title IX violations designed to illustrate the *correct* process to address the investigative process, as well as the discrimination. The following three cases, based on real cases with the names and places changed, show where schools *failed* to address the discrimination correctly and the consequences. All six cases focus on process and analysis. The third section consists of summaries of actual cases where schools were found not to be in compliance and the resolution agreements that resulted. Finally, we close with the exact language OCR requires of schools to adopt 19 different definitions, policies, procedures and protocols. You can take these 19 elements and put your school district's name on them, formally adopt them and have a solid start toward compliance and protection for students and school districts. In addition, you will find other forms and information you are free to use, as well as a journal article we think would be helpful.

Inform yourself and protect your students and your school by complying with Title IX. As experts in Title IX, with extensive backgrounds in law, educational psychology and management, we are here to help. Although we tried to anticipate your questions, no book can offer answers to your specific questions, and this book is no exception to that rule. We invite you to contact us with at the following phone numbers and email addresses. We stand ready to be a resource.

Steve Cohen, Ed.D.
913-927-0229 lmag1@mindspring.com

Larry Altman, JD
314-346-8531 ljalaw@sbcglobal.net

ARE YOU READY?

CHAPTER 1

FEDERAL AND STATE COMPLIANCE—THE BACKSTORY

Public schools in the United States are obligated to do a critically important job for all American children—provide them with a world-class education. Yet, the road to accomplishing this goal has never been easy. Over the years, federal and state laws have added other obligations upon school administrators besides education. For example, some federal statues, such as the Individual with Disabilities Education Act[1] and Section 504 of the Rehabilitation Act 1973[2], mandate that public schools provide a free and appropriate education for students who have qualifying disabilities, alongside their nondisabled peers to the maximum extent possible. And, some federal regulations now require schools to protect students from bullying and sexual harassment. In addition to educating our youth, the most important and precious resource for our country, school administrators must protect all students from unwanted and damaging behaviors. It will be helpful to review some of the federal laws that require public schools to provide our students with a safe environment so that students can receive the great education they deserve.

Condensed History of Laws Protecting Students From Inappropriate Behavior

Since 2010, the Office for Civil Rights has demanded that schools promptly respond to allegations of bullying and harassment, as well as take effective steps to prevent their recurrence. OCR has stated that

---

[1] 20 USC §1400 *et seq.*
[2] 29 USC § 701

when student misconduct violates civil rights laws, not only must the school discipline the perpetrator, it must also "eliminate the hostile environment created by the harassment, address its effects and take steps to ensure that harassment does not recur."[3] This publication, therefore, requires schools to adopt policies that comply with OCR's suggested procedures for conducting investigations of alleged bullying or harassment—or face the potential loss of federal funding.

When reviewing a claim that a school did not take appropriate steps in investigating an allegation of bullying against a student, OCR first focuses upon the process the school used during its investigation of the allegation of bullying or harassment. On October 20, 2013, the Office of Special Education and Rehabilitation Services and the Office of Special Education Programs published a Dear Colleague Letter (DCL) providing public schools with a suggested practice for preventing and addressing bullying.[4] On October 21, 2014, OCR published another DCL informing schools that if a student receiving services under the Individual with Disabilities Education Act[5] or accommodations under Section 504 Rehabilitation Act of 1973[6] is bullied for any reason, even if not related to the child's disability, the school *must determine* whether or not the bullying impacted the child's entitlement to receive a free appropriate public education (FAPE).[7] Thus, federal agencies demand that they expect public schools to teach what they call "clear behavioral expectations" to all students and staff "in the same manner as any core subject."[8]

In response to what it considered to be a national crisis, on April 29, 2014, the Office for Civil Rights published its Questions and Answers on Title IX and Sexual Violence[9]. OCR provided details of what it expects

---

[3] *Dear Colleague Letter,* 55 IDELR 174 (OCR October 26, 2010)

[4] *Dear Colleague Letter,* 113 LRP 35753 (OSERS, August 20, 2013)

[5] 20 USC 1400 *et seq.*

[6] 29 USC § 701

[7] *Dear Colleague Letter: Responding to Bullying of Students with Disabilities* 114 LRP 45954 (OCR October 21, 2014)

[8] *(Dear Colleague Letter* 113 LRP 35753 (OSERS, August 20, 2013)

[9] *Questions and Answers on Title IX and Sexual Violence,* located at http://www2.ed.gov/about/offices/list/ocr/docs/qa-20104-title-ix-pdf.

all public schools to do in cases of sexual violence and sexual harassment so that schools would be in compliance with OCR's interpretation of Title IX, including the requirements for a compliant procedure for the conducting of Title IX investigations. What's more, on May 13, 2016, the Department of Justice (DOJ) and the Department of Education (DOE) published a joint DCL informing schools receiving federal funding that Title IX prohibits discrimination based upon a student's gender identity and prohibits sexual discrimination against transgender students.[10] The administrative branch of the federal government, therefore, has left no doubt that transgender students are entitled to Title IX protection and that gender-identity harassment constitutes illegal discrimination.

That said, there is pushback against the May 2016 publication because of what some consider an abuse of power by the DOJ, DOE and OCR. Last year, two members of the Senate held hearings condemning what they considered an abuse of power by OCR when that agency announced its rules against bullying. So, it would not be a surprise for the head of the Department of Education to come before a Senate committee to discuss what legal authority allowed the DOJ and the DOE to issue its May 2016 document.

Still, one circuit court, the Fourth in *G.G. v. Gloucester County School Board,* 116 LRP 15374 (4th Cir. April 19, 2016), has endorsed the May 2016 directive. The Supreme Court, however, has issued an order that prevents the enforcement of that ruling as court members contemplate allowing an appeal to the Supreme Court to go forward. [11] And, a federal district court judge in Texas has enjoined the Department of Education and the Office for Civil Rights from enforcing the guidelines published on May 13, 2016 against any school district.[12] Until the Supreme Court publishes a determinative ruling regarding Title IX transgender student rights or Congress passes legislation that speaks to this issue, school districts and their attorneys are left with little guidance on the best practice for schools to adopt so that there is compliance with Title IX with regard to

---

[10] Dear Colleague *Letter: Transgender Students* www.ed.gov/letters/colleague-201605-title-ix-transgender.PDF

[11] *G.G. v. Gloucester County School Board,* 116LRP 32968 (Supreme Court, August 3, 2016)

[12] *Texas v. United States,* 116 LRP 35877 (N.D. Tex. August 21, 2016)

transgender students. That said, no court has overruled *Davis v Monroe County Bd. of Educ.* [13] when the Supreme Court ruled that student-on-student sexual harassment could be a violation of Title IX. Therefore, student-on-student sexual harassment and sexual violence are prohibited by Title IX, and schools that fail to address and adequately respond to allegations of sexual harassment and sexual violence could be found to have violated this law.

Federal Agencies Require Schools to Adopt Adequate Protocols and Procedures Against Bullying

OCR has also informed schools that if an IDEA or 504 child is bullied for any reason, even if not related to the child's disability, the school *must determine* whether or not the bullying impacted the child's entitlement to receive a free and appropriate public education (FAPE), if it did, bring together the child's IEP team or 504 committee to address and deal with the impact.[14] This DCL was an "add on" to the April 29, 2014 publication. This publication reminded schools that this guidance also applied to allegations of sexual harassment and sexual violence.

Establishing the Framework for Compliance

Establishing a framework for compliance starts with the creation of policies, protocols and procedures that will meet the goal of full compliance with federal regulations governing complaints connected to bullying and sexual harassment. This requires schools to bring together stakeholders who can discuss the goals for compliance and then develop a plan of action that will lead to the creation of compliant policies, protocols and policies. The stakeholders must include administrative staff that understands the harm caused to students by bullying and sexual harassment, teacher representatives who can illuminate others on the issues they see in the classroom and parent representatives who can explain the issues from a parental point of view and serve as the students' advocates. This not an all-inclusive list because, as the discussions move

---

[13] 526 U.S. 629 (1999)

[14] *Dear Colleague Letter: Responding to Bullying of Students with Disabilities* 114 LRP 45954 (OCR October 21, 2014).

forward, other groups of stakeholders may be identified that must be included so that goals can be met.

Once a plan has been completed, it then must be implemented. And implementation must be supported by all of the stakeholders and the groups they represent. If there is a lack of "buy-in," the implemented plan will fail. After implementation starts, data must be collected to determine whether or not progress has been made towards achieving the goals of compliance and reducing confirmed cases of bullying or sexual harassment. If no progress is shown, that does not mean the plan is a failure. Rather, it is an indication that changes to the plan are required so that progress can be achieved. The stakeholders need to be flexible and ready to change so that ultimately a working, compliant, successful plan that includes the policies, protocols and procedures for the school will be fully implemented.[15]

You are encouraged to take the compliance readiness test in chapter three. It will give you a baseline for comparing your current situation with what is required when you read the questions and answers regarding what schools need to know that follows them. You will also find details and suggestions regarding what school districts might adopt to help them come into compliance with all of the federal requirements.

In the appendix, we have provided policies, protocols and procedures that are yours to take. Feel free to put your school name on them and use them to facilitate compliance. Schools that take the time to update their policies, protocols and procedures to comply with all of the federal and state requirements will be able to create a safer school environment where students can thrive and learn free of harassment, violence and fear.

---

[15] I suggest the reader review the *Baldrige Excellence Builder*, www.nist.gov/baldrige for help in creating compliant policies, protocols, and procedures.

CHAPTER 2

EFFECTS OF BULLYING: RESEARCH AND COMPLIANCE

Imagine a middle school student who suddenly becomes withdrawn or hangs around in a classroom, leaving at the very last minute for the next class. Visualize a child in elementary school who goes from active and social to unusually quiet and passive or the high school student who decides to no longer show up—at all. These issues are all related to harassment in the form of bullying or worse. And we don't have to imagine them because they are, sadly, very real and enough of an issue to have warranted significant research.

HealthDay News has published conclusions from research studies stating that, "The researchers found that kids who are the victims of bullying by peers are more likely to experience anxiety and depression and more likely to hurt themselves as young adults than children who have been mistreated by adults." [16] HealthDay also referred to other research, which found that children involved in bullying are more likely to think about suicide or attempt it than those students who are not subjected to bullying.[17] It should surprise no one that the second leading cause of death for those between the ages of 10 and 24 is suicide.[18]

---

[16] *Bullies and Their Victims May Be At Higher Risk of Suicide"*, Health Day News, January 7, 2015 by Randy Dotinger.

[17] *Bullies and Their Victims May Be At Higher Risk of Suicide"*, Health Day News, January 7, 2015 by Randy Dotinger, referring to a study conducted at the University of Warwick, Coventry, England, co-authored by Dieter Wolke.

[18] Erin P. Sullivan, Joseph L. Annest, Thomas R. Simon, Feijun Luo, Linda L. Dahlberg, *Suicide Trends Among Persons Aged 10-24---United States 1994, 2012,* CENTERS FOR DISEASE CONTROL MORBIDITY AND MORTALITY WEEKLY REPORT (March 6, 2015), available at http://www.cdc.gov/mmwr/preview/mmwrhtml/mm6408al.htm.

Even before the publication of these reports, the Office of Special Education and Rehabilitative Services Offices of Special Education Programs published a Dear Colleague Letter[19] (DCL) informing schools that bullying would undermine a student's ability to achieve his or her full academic potential. Worse, the DCL said that students who are bullied would also feel alienated from school, loneliness or depression.

In addition, the Office for Civil Rights has informed schools that if a disabled student has been subjected to bullying or harassment due to his/her disability, there is a strong likelihood that the student's ability to be provided a free appropriate public education (FAPE) will be impacted.[20] When bullying against a disabled student occurs, schools must promptly determine whether or not the student's educational needs are still being met and, if not, make prompt changes to the student's individual education or 504 plan, so that the student can continue to receive FAPE.

On January 16, 2015 OCR's San Francisco office informed schools that when a disabled student is bullied, for any reason, the school must determine what happened and then take steps to prevent recurrence.[21] In Huntington Beach City an IDEA (Individuals with Disabilities Act) Jewish student complained that he was being harassed by other students who were using negative stereotypes about Jews and being bullied for reasons not related to his disability or religion. The position of DOE and OCR is that bullying of any disabled student for any reason, even if unrelated to the student's disability, must be investigated and, if confirmed, corrected.

The student said that the school did not take appropriate steps to investigate his allegations nor did the school take appropriate steps to end the harassment and bullying. He stated that he was left to respond to the harassment and bullying inappropriately, which then caused him to be disciplined. In addition, he claimed that the harassment and bullying

---

[19] 113 LRP 3753 (OSERS, August 13,2013)

[20] *Dear Colleague Letter: Responding to Bullying of Students with Disabilities* 114 LRP 45954 (OCR October 21, 2014).

[21] (*Huntington Beach City (CA) School District,* 115 LRP 17622 (Office for Civil Rights, Western Division, San Francisco (California), January 16, 2015)

caused him to experience emotional trauma. OCR informed the school that it had an obligation to investigate the allegations, and, if confirmed, take steps to prevent recurrence and provide assistance to the victim.

In fact, failure to take these steps, including the failure to provide assistance to help the victim deal with his emotional trauma, was a potential violation of federal law. This sounds very compliance-based for a reason. If the school had been in compliance and staff had been trained as required, the damage to this student could have been avoided—the ultimate goal. It's easy to imagine this scenario because the reality of bullying plays out in many schools regardless of the disability, ethnicity, age or religion. Allegations need to be investigated, so that prevention and protection can be implemented when needed.

In this case, OCR found that the school did not do enough to investigate whether or not a hostile environment existed, did not provide staff enough training and did not assess whether or not, as a result of the bullying, the student's educational needs changed requiring the school to provide additional services to the student. Accordingly, the school entered into a resolution agreement to correct the deficiencies.

Bullying crosses geographic, age and socio-economic lines and can range from verbal to cyber to assault. The research and example given here are just a few of the reasons for the extensive involvement of the federal government directive to public schools to put an end to the many issues caused by bullying and create a school environment that is "positive, safe, and nurturing,"[22] so that students are safe and emotional issues and the horror of student suicide due to bullying and harassment become a thing of the past.

---

[22] Dear Colleague Letter, 113 LRP 33753 (OSERS, August 13, 2013)

CHAPTER 3

TITLE IX READINESS TEST

What follows is a quick evaluation of your current knowledge and level of compliance.

1. Did you know that the federal court standards for Title IX compliance are not the same as the OCR's standards?
   Yes_____ No_____

In the Davis v Monroe (February 1999) case, the court created a deliberate indifference standard to prove school liability and obtain monetary damages under Title IX. This requires a plaintiff to prove that school officials had actual knowledge of the pervasive and severe sexual harassment or violence.

On the other hand, OCR has indicated in its guidance (April 29, 2014) that it will conclude that a school has violated a student's Title IX right to be free of sexual harassment if it determines that the school knew or *should have known:*

- About the bullying or harassment.
- The bullying or harassment was pervasive.
- The bullying and harassment interferes with or limits the student's participation in the educational opportunities.

If the school doesn't stop this, it opens itself up to a claim of negligence.

Therefore: Your school must be in compliance with both the federal court and OCR.

2. Did you know that transgender students and international students are specifically protected by Title IX and that your school district or university has specific obligations to provide them special protections? Yes_____No_____

3. Do you provide the additional protections required under Title IX specifically for transgender and international students? Yes _____ No_____ Don't know_____

4. Do you provide training for all your students that informs them that they are forbidden under Title IX from making threats of deportation to international students? Yes_____No_____ Don't know_____

OCR states that all students from elementary to professional school, along with male, female, straight, gay, lesbian, bisexual, *transgender,* full-time, part-time, disabled, nondisabled, different races and national origins are protected by Title IX. In addition, *international students,* regardless of their immigration status, and including undocumented students, are protected. This requires schools to make certain that all reporting forms and training sessions are given in the language that the international student understands.

OCR specifically says that schools must take additional steps to protect transgender and international students. They require schools to train faculty and staff about working with LGBT and gender nonconforming students. Additionally, OCR says that schools must make certain that its faculty and staff are capable of providing *culturally competent counseling* to all victims of sexual violence.

OCR also requires schools to allow foreign students on a student visa who are victims of sexual violence or sexual harassment to drop below full-time caseloads. OCR mandates that schools must specifically protect international students from threats of deportation, as such a threat may be used to deter international students from reporting Title IX complaints.

Schools must specifically inform alleged perpetrators that threats that may deter the international student from making a Title IX complaint would be a violation of Title IX's rules against retaliation. This means that schools are required to provide specific training for all students because any one of them might become an alleged perpetrator.

5. Did you know that under the OCR Title, IX interacts with IDEA and Section 504 of the Rehabilitation Act?
Yes_____No_____

6. Do you formally consider the application of IDEA and 504 remedies when focusing on a student who has been the victim of bullying or sexual violence?
Yes_____No_____Don't know_____

OCR says that students who previously required no IDEA or 504 accommodations might, as a result of being a victim of sexual violence, need IDEA services or 504 accommodations.

In addition, OCR states that victims of sexual violence may develop mental health disabilities "that should be addressed and might require schools to provide the student with special education services or reasonable accommodations."

Both laws require schools to locate and evaluate all students suspected of having a disability to determine whether or not the student requires special education services. It is the student being a victim of sexual violence that triggers a school's Child Find obligations.

On October 21, 2014, OCR made it mandatory for all schools to consider the impact that bullying, sexual harassment or sexual violence has upon a victimized disabled child's ability to receive FAPE under the IDEA or 504.

Schools must consider:

- Whether or not there has been a sudden decline in grades.
- Whether or not there has been the onset of emotional outburst or emotional withdrawal by the student.
- Whether or not the student has exhibited an increase in the frequency or intensity of classroom behavioral interrupting or

a decrease in classroom participation or a change in personal hygiene.

- Whether or not the student has shown a rise in missed days, lateness coming to class, skipped classes, frequent trips to the nurse's office or refusal to accept IEP services.

7. Did you know that OCR has mandated specific elements be included in your training programs. A partial list includes:

- All faculty and staff must be trained on the requirements of confidentiality when dealing with incidents of sexual violence.
- All staff must be trained on how to prevent and identify sexual violence and sexual harassment.
- All staff training must include what attitudes of bystanders may allow sexual violence and sexual harassment to continue.
- All staff must be trained regarding how to respond to a student's request for confidentiality.

Does your faculty and staff training include all these elements?

Yes_____ No_____ Some of them_____ Don't know_____

8. Did you know that OCR wants **all** your students trained? A *partial* list of specific topics required by OCR includes:

- What constitutes sexual violence and sexual harassment.
- How the school will determine whether or not the conduct was, under Title IX, unacceptable.
- How the school will determine whether or not illegal sexual conduct creates a hostile sexual environment.
- The school's reporting options, school time frames and confidential disclosure options.
- The effects of trauma on the victim, including neurobiological.
- Strategies and skills for bystanders to intervene and prevent possible sexual violence.

There are more required elements, but for the sake of this test, does your student training include the listed elements?

Yes_____ No_____ Some of them_____ Don't know_____

9. Did you know that your school must take interim measures to protect students once the school is put on notice that sexual violence or sexual harassment has occurred?

   Yes_____ No_____

10. Have you adopted these interim measures?

    Yes_____ No_____ Don't know_____

11. Did you know that perpetrators must receive rehabilitative training?

    Yes_____ No_____

12. If the answer to number 11 is yes, do you provide it?

    Yes_____ No_____ Don't know_____

OCR mandates that interim measures to protect the alleged victim must be put into place *immediately* upon receiving the complaint. The interim measures specified under Title IX include:

- School must inform the alleged victim that he/she has the right to avoid contact with the alleged perpetrator and from illegal retaliation.
- The school must allow the alleged victim to change academic and extracurricular activities.
- The school must allow the alleged victim to change his/her living, dining and transportation conditions.
- If requested, the school must provide an escort to the alleged victim so he/she can move about the school without the chance of being caught and exposed to retaliation by the alleged perpetrator or his/her surrogates.

13. Have you read and are you conversant with the April 29, 2014 OCR "Dear Colleague" mandates?

    Yes_____ No_____

So, how many of these questions did you answer correctly? If you missed or didn't know any of them, the critical question becomes: How out of compliance are you—really?

The final question is whether or not you want to risk the multitude of compliance requirements not contained here. *The answer is no—read on.*

CHAPTER 4

QUESTIONS AND ANSWERS ON TITLE IX AND SEXUAL VIOLENCE 114 LRP19550 OFFICE FOR CIVIL RIGHTS

I. **Introduction**

On April 29, 2014, in response to what it considered to be a national crisis, the Office for Civil Rights published its Questions and Answers on Title IX and Sexual Violence, 114 LRP 19550. Although OCR claimed that this publication was nothing more than clarification of its position regarding how it will enforce Title IX, in reality OCR provided details of what it expects all public schools to do in cases of sexual violence and in other forms of sexual harassment so that schools would be in compliance with OCR's interpretation of Title IX. What follows is a summation of highlights of the publication.

II. **School's Obligation to Respond to Sexual Violence**

A. Definition of Sexual Violence

    1. Physical sexual acts perpetrated against a person's will or where a person is unable to give consent because of the person's age, intellectual disability or due to the use of drugs or alcohol.

B. Sexual violence can be carried out by school employees, other students or third parties.

C. Schools violate Title IX when:

    1. The alleged conduct is sufficiently serious to limit or deny a student's ability to participate in, or benefit from, the school's educational program, **and**

2. Upon notice, the school fails to take prompt, effective steps reasonably calculated to end the sexual violence, eliminate the hostile environment, prevent its recurrence and, as appropriate, remedy its effect upon the victim and other students.

D. OCR requires an evaluation of the conduct from the perspective of a reasonable person **in the alleged victim's position.**

E. The more severe the conduct, the less need there is to show a repetitive series of incidents to prove a hostile environment, particularly if the conduct is physical.

F. A school has notice of sexual violence if a responsible employee knew or, in the exercise of reasonable care, should have known about the sexual violence.

1. If a school could have learned about the sexual violence by making a "proper" inquiry, OCR will impute knowledge upon the school.

2. A school's delay or failure to respond to an allegation of sexual violence creates an illegal hostile environment.

G. Child Find obligations under IDEA and Section 504.

1. Students who previously required no IDEA services or 504 accommodations may, as a result of being a victim of sexual violence, need IDEA services or 504 accommodations. Child Find obligations of both laws, therefore, are triggered after a student is a victim of sexual violence.

III. All Students Are Protected by Title IX

A. All students in schools receiving any federal funding, from elementary to postsecondary schools, including male, female, straight, gay, lesbian, bisexual, transgender, full-time, part-time, disabled and nondisabled, as well as different races and national origins are protected by Title IX.

B. Title IX extends to claims of discrimination based upon gender identity or failure to conform to stereotypical notions of masculinity or femininity.

C. Schools must train school counselors and staff responsible for reporting and investigating complaints of sexual violence about working with LGBT and gender nonconforming students, along with same-sex sexual violence.

D. International students, regardless of immigration status, including undocumented students, are protected by Title IX.

IV. Overview of Title IX Procedural Requirements

A. Each school **must**:

1. Publish a notice of nondiscrimination that states:

   a. The school does not discriminate on the basis of sex in its educational programs and activities as required by Title IX.

   b. Questions regarding Title IX may be referred to the school's Title IX coordinator or to OCR.

   c. The designated Title IX coordinator's name or title, email and office addresses and phone number.

2. Designate at least one employee to coordinate the school's efforts to comply with and carry out its responsibilities under Title IX. This person will be known as the school's Title IX coordinator.

3. Adopt and publish Title IX grievance procedures that provide for the prompt and equitable resolution of student and employee sex discrimination complaints, including, but not limited to, allegations of sexual violence.

4. Provide all sexual violence reporting forms, information and training so they are accessible to all students and employees, including English language learners and the disabled, keeping in mind that Title IX protects all students at recipient schools regardless of national origin, immigration or citizenship status.

V. Title IX Coordinator Responsibilities

A. Oversee the school's response to Title IX reports and complaints.

B. Identify and address any patterns or systemic problems revealed by the complaints.

C. Be informed of **all** reports and complaints arising under Title IX, even when the complaint or report was initially filed with another school employee and even when someone other than the Title IX coordinator is conducting the investigation.

D. If a school uses its disciplinary procedures as part of its obligations to comply with Title IX, the Title IX coordinator must review those procedures to make certain they comply with the prompt and equitable requirements of Title IX.

E. The Title IX coordinator must receive training to carry out his/her duties.

F. The Title IX coordinator must receive the authority and visibility to fulfill his/her duties.

G. The Title IX coordinator cannot be the same person who would represent the school in legal claims alleging Title IX violations against the school.

VI. **Title IX Grievance Procedures:** OCR will review **all** aspects of a school's policies and practices. Those include, but are not limited to, mandatory school grievance procedures. OCR requires that the following be included in all schools' grievance procedures:

A. A statement of the school's jurisdiction over Title IX complaints.

B. Definitions of sexual harassment and sexual violence.

C. An explanation of when sexual harassment or sexual violence creates a hostile environment.

D. Reporting policies and protocols.

E. Provisions for confidential reporting.

F. Identification of the employees responsible for evaluating requests for confidentiality.

G. Notice that Title IX prohibits retaliation.

H. Notice of the student's right to simultaneously file a Title IX and criminal complaint.

I. Notice of the interim measures to take to protect a complainant in the educational setting.

J. Notice that the evidentiary standard that a school must take in determining whether or not the allegations are true shall be by a preponderance of the evidence. OCR says that this means the evidence must show that more likely than not sexual violence or harassment did occur and that more likely than not the perpetrator committed the act.

K. Notice of potential remedies for the victim.

L.   Notice of the potential sanctions that can be taken against the perpetrator.

M. Sources of counseling, advocacy and support for the victim.

N. Notice to students, parents of elementary and secondary students and employees where complaints may be filed.

O. Notice to students, parents of elementary and secondary students and employees of the school's grievance procedures.

P.   Notice to students, parents of elementary and secondary students and employees of how the grievance procedure applies to complaints filed by students or complaints filed on their behalf.

Q. Provisions for adequate, reliable and impartial investigation of complaints, including, but not limited to, the opportunity for the complainant and the alleged perpetrator to present witnesses and evidence.

R. Designated and reasonable prompt time frames for completion of the major stages of the complaint process.

S. Written notice to the complainant and the alleged perpetrator of the outcome of the complaint.

T.   Written assurance that the school will take steps to prevent recurrence of any sexual violence and, when appropriate, remedy the discriminatory effects on the complainant and other students.

VII. Responsible Employees and Title IX Reporting Obligations

A. Responsible employees are persons who have authority to take actions to redress sexual violence or who have the duty of reporting incidents of sexual violence or any misconduct of students to the Title IX coordinator or other school employee or whom a student could reasonably believe has the authority to report incidents of sexual violence.

    1. In reality, this is every employee of the school.

B. Reporting employees must be told:

    1. Of their reporting obligations.

    2. To whom they should report.

    3. Their obligation to inform complainants of the employee's obligation to report allegations of sexual violence.

4. Their obligation to inform complainants of their option to request confidentiality and about the availability of confidential advocacy, counseling or other support services and the right to file a Title IX complaint with the school and to report a crime to law enforcement.

    a. An elementary student may reasonably believe that a custodial staff person or cafeteria staff person is an appropriate person for the student to approach with a complaint, but a college student should know that these employees would not have the authority to act. Thus, college students would be expected not to take their complaints of sexual violence to custodial staff or dining hall employees.

C. When a responsible employee knows or reasonably should know of possible sexual violence, OCR deems that a school has notice and must take immediate and appropriate steps to investigate and determine what in fact occurred.

D. Responsible employees must report the following information about a possible incident of sexual violence:

    1. Names, if known, of the alleged perpetrators.
    2. The name of the student who experienced the alleged act of sexual violence.
    3. The relevant facts, including, but not limited to, the time, date and location of the alleged assault.
    4. Names, if known, of witnesses to the incident.

E. After a student tells an employee that he/she was the victim of sexual violence, the responsible employee must inform the student, before the student discloses information that the student wants confidential, that:

    1. The employee has a mandatory obligation to report the names of the alleged perpetrators and victim involved in the alleged act of sexual violence, along with all relevant facts to the school's Title IX coordinator or other appropriate school officials.

2. That the student does have the right to request confidentiality that the school's Title IX coordinator or other appropriate school official will consider.

3. The student's ability to share confidential information with counselors or advocacy, health, mental health or sexual violence related services such as sexual violence resource centers, pastoral counselors and campus mental health centers.

VIII. Confidentiality Versus a School's Obligation to Respond to Sexual Violence

A. If a student requests that his/her name not be disclosed to the alleged perpetrator or that the school not investigate the allegations, the school must:

1. Inform the student that honoring the request may limit the school's ability to respond to the incident, including, but not limited to, pursuing disciplinary action against the alleged perpetrator.

2. Inform the student that Title IX includes protection against retaliation.

3. Inform the student that it will take steps to prevent retaliation, and if retaliation does occur, the school will take "strong" responsive action.

B. After providing this information, if the student still requests confidentiality, the school must determine whether or not it can honor the request and still provide all students with a safe environment. The factors the school must consider when determining whether or not to honor this request are:

1. Circumstances that the alleged perpetrator may commit additional acts of violence or sexual violence.

   a. Schools will need to investigate whether or not the alleged perpetrator has a prior history of violence.

   b. Schools will also need to investigate whether or not the alleged perpetrator threatened the victim not to proceed with a complaint.

2. Schools will need to investigate whether or not the alleged act reveals a pattern of misconduct, such as

the use of illegal drugs or alcohol to subdue the victim, and whether or not there is a location pattern or that a particular group has been sexually assaulting students.

    3. Schools must also consider:

        a. Whether or not a weapon was used.

        b. The age of the alleged victim.

        c. The mental competency of the alleged victim.

        d. Whether or not the school has alternatives to obtain evidence of the alleged attack, such as security cameras, witness reports or physical evidence.

C. If the school decides it must disclose the name of the alleged victim to the alleged perpetrator, it must first inform the alleged victim before making the disclosure.

D. If the school determines that it must disclose the alleged victim's name to the alleged perpetrator, the school must take necessary interim steps to protect the alleged victim and to protect the safety of all students.

IX. Investigations and Hearings of Title IX Complaints

A. In investigating a complaint, the school must determine:

    1. Whether or not the misconduct occurred.

    2. If the misconduct did occur, what actions the school will take to end the sexual violence and, if it exists, eliminate the hostile environment and prevent recurrence. This may include:

        a. Imposing sanctions on the perpetrator.

        b. Providing remedies for the complainant and the broader student population.

B. The investigation must be adequate, reliable, impartial and prompt, allowing both parties to present witnesses and other evidence.

C. Additional OCR requirements:

    1. If the school permits one party to have an attorney or advisor present at any stage of the proceeding, it must allow the other side the same right.

2. If the school permits one party to submit third-party, expert testimony, it must allow the other party the same right.

3. If a school conducts a hearing and an appeal process is permitted, both parties must have the right of appeal.

4. Must notify both parties in writing of the outcome of the complaint and of any decision made after a hearing and an appeal to that hearing.

D. Hearings:

1. Hearings are not mandatory.

2. If a school does conduct hearings to determine whether or not an act of sexual violence occurred, then:

   a. If the school permits cross-examination of witnesses, including the parties, both sides must be permitted the same opportunity, except:

      i. OCR discourages schools from allowing parties to personally question or cross-examine each other during a hearing on alleged sexual violence. Instead, schools may allow the parties to submit questions to the hearing officer of the panel to ask questions on their behalf. Also, OCR recommends that this party screen out any inappropriate or irrelevant questions.

3. If the school permits one party to be present for a hearing, it must allow all parties to be present for the hearing.

4. The complainant's previous sexual history with anyone other the alleged perpetrator is not permitted.

5. A finding of a previous consensual dating or sexual relationship between the parties does not in of itself preclude a finding that sexual violence did occur.

6. Conduct hearings in a manner that does not inflict additional trauma on the complainant.

X. **Interaction with Criminal Investigation**

A. The termination of a criminal investigation without an arrest or conviction does not end the school's Title IX obligations.

B. A school cannot wait for the conclusion of a criminal investigation to begin or complete its own Title IX investigation.

XI. Off-Campus Conduct

A. A school must process all complaints of sexual violence no matter where it occurred and must determine:
   1. Whether or not the misconduct occurred in the context of an educational program or activity, or
   2. Had an effect on campus or off-campus education programs or activities.

B. If the school determines that either of the above has occurred, it must treat and investigate the alleged act exactly as it would if the misconduct occurred on campus.

C. Off-campus programs are not limited to activities that take place in fraternity or sorority houses, school-sponsored field trips, including athletic team travel, and off-campus events for school clubs.

D. Once a school is on notice of off-campus sexual violence against a student, it must assess whether or not there are any continuing effects off-campus or contributing to a hostile environment.

E. Schools must protect students from off-campus sexual perpetrators in the same way it would protect the students if the perpetrator were on campus.

XII. Time Frames

A. OCR requires that from start to finish, the "typical" investigation into a complaint of sexual violence should be 60 days. Included in this time frame are:
   1. Conducting the fact-finding investigation.
   2. Holding a hearing or engaging in another decision-making process to determine whether or not the alleged misconduct occurred and whether or not a hostile environment exists.
   3. Determining what actions the school should take to eliminate the hostile environment and prevent a recurrence, including, but not limited to, imposing sanctions upon the perpetrator and providing remedies

       to the complainant and, as needed, to the entire school community.

B. The time frame does not include the appeal process, but OCR will not allow what it considers to be an unduly long appeal process.

C. The 60 days is not a hard and fixed timeline and does recognize that the time to complete the process may take longer because of school breaks or if a parallel criminal investigation is also taking place.

XIII. Interim Measures

A. Before completion of an investigation into an allegation of sexual violence, the school must take steps to protect the alleged victim that include, but are not limited to:

    1. Ensuring that the victim continues to have equal access to the school's educational programs and activities.

    2. Protecting the student from the alleged perpetrator and from illegal retaliation.

B. The school must inform the alleged victim of his/her right to avoid contact with the alleged perpetrator and allow the alleged victim to change academic and extracurricular activities, along with changing the student's living, transportation, dining and working situation.

C. When taking interim measures, OCR requires schools to minimize the burden upon the alleged victim.

XIV. Remedies and Notice of Outcome

A. OCR requires that all services needed to remedy the hostile environment be offered to the victim.

B. Remedies may include:

    1. Disciplinary action against the perpetrator.

    2. Providing counseling services for the perpetrator.

    3. Changes to the school's overall services and policies.

    4. Targeted training for a group of students to remedy a hostile environment—for example, an athletic team or band.

    5. Remedies for the victim may include, but are not limited to:

       a. Providing an escort for the victim to make certain that the victim can move safely between classes and activities.

       b. Moving the perpetrator to a different residence hall or, in the case of an elementary or secondary school, to another school within the same district.

          i. Accommodating the victim if he/she requests a move.

       c. Providing at no cost to the victim, comprehensive victim services including, but not limited to, medical assistance, counseling, academic support and, if needed, tutoring.

       d. Arranging for the victim, without academic or financial penalty, to have extra time to complete or retake a class or withdraw from a class.

6. These remedies are separate from, and in addition to, any interim measures that may have been offered or provided prior to the conclusion of the investigation. In the event the victim did not take advantage of a specific service, the victim is still entitled to and should be reoffered any appropriate final remedies previously declined.

C. Title IX requires that the school notify, in writing, all parties about the outcome of the complaint. If the school confirms the allegations, the school must not inform the perpetrator of the remedies offered or provided to the victim.

1. If the allegations are confirmed, then the school must inform the victim of the sanctions taken against the perpetrator that "directly" relate to the victim, the remedies being offered to the victim, the steps the school will take to prevent recurrence and, if the school finds that a hostile environment exists, the steps it is taking to eliminate the hostile environment.

XV. Appeals

A. OCR does not mandate an appeal process, however, OCR recommends that schools have an appeal process in place where procedural error or previously unavailable evidence is discovered that may significantly impact the outcome or where a sanction is substantially disproportionate to the findings.

    1. But OCR provides no guidance on what it means by the phrases, "significantly impact" or "substantially disproportionate to the findings."

B. If an appeal process is in place, both parties must have equal access.

XVI. Training for Staff and Students

A. Topics for training **all staff** that OCR wants covered:

    1. The appropriate people to whom they are to report about incidents of sexual violence.

        a. For example, the "responsible employees of the district" and the "Title IX coordinator."

    2. That they **must** report sexual violence to appropriate school officials **and** that there are consequences for failing to do so.

    3. Requirements regarding confidentiality when dealing with incidents of sexual violence.

    4. How to prevent and identify sexual violence, including, but not limited to, same-sex sexual violence.

    5. What behaviors may result or lead to acts of sexual violence.

    6. What attitudes of bystanders may allow sexual violence to continue.

    7. How to appropriately respond to a student who may have been the victim of sexual violence, including the use of nonjudgmental language when talking to the alleged victim and how to deal with the trauma that the victim might be experiencing.

    8. How to respond to a student's request to keep the incident confidential.

    9. That they must, in all cases, provide the victim contact information for the school's Title IX coordinator.

B. Staff training must occur on a "regular basis," and there must be "a method for verifying whether or not the training was effective."

C. Training for what the OCR refers to as Responsible Employees of the District

    1. All staff with authority to address sexual violence must learn how to appropriately respond to reports of sexual assault.

    2. How to inform victims of the school's obligations to investigate the allegations.

    3. How to inform victims of their option to maintain confidentiality, their right to obtain confidential advocacy, counseling or other support services offered by the school, their right to file a Title IX complaint with the school and the right to report a crime to school or local law enforcement.

D. Topics OCR recommends during training of students. The exact form of the training shall be adjusted, depending upon the age of the students, and schools should consider offering this training to parents in addition to their children.

    1. Title IX and what constitutes sexual violence, including, but not limited to same-sex sexual violence.

    2. The school's definition of consent applicable to sexual conduct, including examples:

        a. This may not be required for schools K through 12.

    3. How the school will determine whether or not conduct was, under Title IX, unacceptable.

    4. How the school will determine whether or not illegal sexual conduct creates a hostile environment.

    5. Reporting options, including, but not limited to, reporting of alleged sexual violence, confidential disclosure options and school time frames, if any, for reporting the alleged incident.

    6. The grievance procedures used by the school to report complaints of sexual violence.

    7. The school's disciplinary provisions relating to sexual violence and the consequences for violating policy.

    8. Effects of trauma on the victim, including neurobiological changes.

9. The role that alcohol and drugs play, including, but not limited to, the deliberate use of alcohol or drugs to perpetrate the sexual violence.

10. Strategies and skills for bystanders to intervene and prevent possible sexual violence.

11. The student's right to pursue law enforcement proceedings at the same time as proceeding with a Title IX grievance.

12. Title IX's protection against retaliation.

13. Encouraging students to report sexual violence.

14. Informing students to whom they should report if an act of sexual violence occurs.

15. Informing students to whom they may speak, in confidence, about an act of sexual violence, and whom the student may speak to who can provide the student with resources regarding victim advocacy, housing assistance, academic support, counseling, disability services, health and mental health services and legal assistance.

16. Provide students with the name of the Title IX coordinator and advise that they report any acts of sexual violence to this individual. When this person is informed, he/she will receive the names of alleged perpetrator, the victim, the relevant facts of the incident including, but not limited to, the time, date and location. Must tell students of the efforts the school will make to comply with the victim's request for confidentiality.

XVII. Conclusion

OCR has put schools on notice that it expects them to provide a thorough review of all complaints of sexual violence. Further, any school that elects to ignore or dismiss claims of sexual violence without a thorough review will face sanctions from OCR. In addition, the requirements contained in the April 29th publication should be factored into any Title IX claim, not just claims of sexual violence Thus the April 29th OCR's publication is another federal mandate that requires prompt action from all schools receiving federal funding.

WHAT COULD HAPPEN

INTRODUCTION

It's important to look at actual cases—which we do in the next section—but there are aspects of compliance to address that we believe would be well served by cases that directly illuminate specific aspects of compliance. Our lengthy and multifaceted experience in the field of Title IX compliance enables to present cases that highlight what to do, and what not to do, when it comes to compliance.

The first three cases are relatively lengthy and hypothetical, as they showcase the investigative process, which is "the other half" of compliance. They look at effective interviewing and directional investigating where schools *did it right*. If you don't pay attention to the follow-through of allegations, you can set yourself up for some serious complications and consequences. The purpose, more than diversity of allegation or age of the student, is to show how to thoroughly and correctly investigate an allegation, a significant part of being in compliance.

Following these three cases are summaries of situations where schools were not in compliance. At this point, there is no need to present the investigative process in detail, so they are set up with the need-to-know information bulleted and brief, for the purpose of showing what the schools did wrong. You will quickly see the case, what was done and what was not done, resulting in noncompliance.

All six cases include a conclusion to clarify and analyze the right and the wrong of compliance. In the first three cases, the conclusions are set up as a continuation of the case to help with handling the process of investigation correctly. The conclusions in the second three cases take a more "lessons to be learned" approach.

CHAPTER 5

CASE STUDY—SEVENTH GRADE

A seventh grade student at Longfellow Middle School, Shelby is mildly autistic and mainstreamed into a regular class. She is a happy girl, who is likable in many ways.

One day, she was lined up with others in her class to go to the cafeteria when one of her classmates, the boy standing directly behind her, reached around and poked her in the ribs. As Shelby turned around to see who did this, the boy, Donald Greene, snickered at her. The touching incident was startling to Shelby. She was not ticklish but wasn't sure what to think about it or how to process what had just happened to her. She was, however, a bit irritated by the incident. The incident was not witnessed by Shelby's teacher, and none of her classmates viewed the incident as problematic. Shelby did not say anything to her teacher or her parents about the incident. Her parents, who were highly tuned into Shelby, picked something up from her mood and surmised that something was bothering her. Because of her mild autism, she could not express herself well enough to provide her parents with much information.

A few days later, the incident repeated itself. The same boy, Donald Greene, lined up behind Shelby. They were at the very end of the line, and he took the opportunity to poke her again. This time it was higher up and closer in toward Shelby's breasts. She was again startled, and when she turned to face the person who did this, she discovered it was the same boy as before. This time his expression was even less friendly. Shelby did not like being touched, and her parents had made it a point to teach her not to allow others to touch her. Standing up for herself was not an easy thing for Shelby, as she was shy and aware that she was not like the other kids. Her mood started to turn "dark," and now it was apparent to even her teacher that something was wrong. Shelby could not articulate what was bothering her, and her parents were starting to become concerned.

A week later, while the class lined up to go out, Donald Greene again lined up behind Shelby. Again, they were at the end of the line. This time he grabbed her at her waist with both of his hands and drew her rear-end into his groin, making rubbing movements while he held her against him. This was observed by two other students in the class and reported to the teacher. Shelby was horrified by the incident. She was very agitated, and her mother had to be called. The teacher questioned Shelby, Donald and the others, then filled out an incident report.

Shelby is now refusing to go to school and cries when the subject is brought up by her mother.

Questions:

- Were Title IX regulations violated?
- Which one or ones (if any)?
- What should the school administration do? Whom should be interviewed and in what order?
- What interim steps (if any) should be taken?
- What conclusions should be reached?
- What recommended actions should be taken?

Were Title IX regulations violated?

The answer is yes.

Which ones?

The behavior demonstrated by Donald Greene meets OCR's definition of sexual violence: "Physical sexual acts perpetrated against a person's will or where a person is unable to give consent because of the person's age, intellectual disability, or due to the use of drugs or alcohol."

Hostile Sexual Environment: A hostile sexual environment exists when "conduct of a sexual nature is severe, persistent or pervasive so as to limit a student's ability to participate in or benefit from the educational program or to create a hostile or abusive environment." This cannot be banter but, rather, persistent or pervasive misconduct that has the effect of limiting the student's ability to participate in or benefit from the educational program offered by the school. In this case, the behavior was severe.

What should the school administration do? Who should be interviewed and in what order?

Since it has been determined that Title IX regulations have been violated and, more importantly, that the student, Shelby, has been traumatized, legally and ethically something formal must be done. Additionally, what is done must be thorough and timely. Thorough means thorough—every relevant person must be interviewed, and timely means it must start and end within a specified timetable. In fact, Title IX regulations indicate a specific course of action to be taken.

The first thing to do is to determine if the alleged victim or perpetrator is already receiving services or accommodations under the Individuals with Disabilities Education Act (IDEA) or 504. IDEA and 504 require their own set of responses. Within 24 hours, the school must start taking action that includes consideration of interim measures to protect Shelby even before the incident is formally investigated. The regulations specify that the investigation must be concluded within 60 days and that specific steps be taken.

What interim measures could be taken and, under Title IX, must be considered?

Any or all of the following could represent appropriate interim measures: class changes for either party (the alleged victim or the alleged perpetrator), waiving or modifying school policies or requirements or providing an escort between classes. Once the school and Shelby's parents are satisfied that, for the present, Shelby is protected, then the investigation should begin. When the alleged victim is a minor, the first interview is always with the alleged victim's teacher. The typical questions are the following:

- Generally speaking, what kind of person is Shelby (shy, happy, sad, withdrawn, extraverted, etc.)?
- Is it in Shelby's character to overreact to things?
- How does Shelby usually deal with stress?
- How resilient is Shelby?
- Are there any other students who should be interviewed who could shed light on Shelby's or Donald's character?

The next thing to do with the alleged victim's teacher is to establish a baseline on Shelby's school related behavior—i.e. current grades, hygiene status, social status, etc. The reason for this is to have something against which to monitor her future status. The school must monitor Shelby for a three-month period following the incident to see if there is any deterioration in her status as a result of the incident. Do her grades decline? Does she continue to maintain her physical appearance? Does she withdraw from her friends? What is her physical stamina and endurance? If there are appreciable declines, then further steps must be taken to restore her to her previous status.

The next interview is with Shelby and her mother (or father or both). In this instance, it is known that the incident occurred because there were witnesses to the fact. The interviewer should direct his or her questions to both the parent and to Shelby. After an initial rapport is established, the following questions should be asked, and Shelby's mother can provide answers if Shelby cannot, due to her autism:

- Shelby, can you tell me if Donald is a friend of yours?
- Can you tell me what happened to you?
- Can you tell me how it makes you feel?
- Did the incident make you annoyed or upset, offended or threatened or terrified? With this question, we are trying to understand the depth of Shelby's feeling.

The next interview is with the alleged perpetrator's teacher. The interviewer should ask:

- What kind of student is Donald Greene?

- What kind of person is he?
- Who are his friends? Are they a good influence on Donald or not?
- What kind of home life might he have?
- Is there anything in his character that causes the teacher to worry about Donald's choices?
- Are there any other students who should be interviewed who might shed light on Donald's character?

The alleged perpetrator's teacher has, or should have, lots of insights worth gathering. In addition, the teacher should be sensitized to watch Donald very closely.

The next interview should be with Donald Greene and his mother (or father or both). Because he is a minor, his parents or guardians should be included in the process. The questions he should be asked include the following:

- Why did you touch Shelby the way you did?
- Do you like Shelby?
- Have you touched Shelby at any time in the past?
- Have you touched any other students like you touched Shelby in the past?
- Do you think it was wrong to do what you did to Shelby?
- What do you think the consequences of touching Shelby that way should be?
- What kind of person are you?
- Do you have any friends who would or could tell anything about you (your character)?

The next set of interviews should be with witnesses to the incident. The witnesses are basically other students who were bystanders. They should be asked the following:

- Tell me, what did you see?
- Tell me what you saw Donald do.
- Tell me what you saw Shelby do.
- What was Shelby's reaction to what was happening to her?

The last set of interviews should be the character witnesses who were suggested by the teachers. These students probably did not witness the incident between Donald and Shelby, but they do have insight into what kind of people they are and what their characters are like. The investigator should be interested in figuring out if this incident was an isolated case or part of a pattern of behavior. A subtler question is, "Is this the beginning of a pattern?"

As a matter of the Title IX rules and as a matter of morality as an educational administrator, you do not want to see Shelby (or any other student) victimized. OCR's requirement is that the school take steps to see that the micro incident not be underreacted to, as well as not repeated in the future (toward Shelby or toward other students).

To return to the matter of bystanders, OCR demands that schools adopt a philosophy and strategy for bystanders to intervene in situations like this one. This is one of the elements in OCR's regulations that has the potential for a culture or paradigm shift, not only in school but also in society at large. It is simply not enough for students to get out their smartphones and make a video of an incident of bullying or worse. That is passive and completely misses the point of demonstrating compassion.

Again, while it is very true that in a capitalistic system, the business setting is very Darwinistic (only the strong survive), schools should not be Darwinistic! And, an evolved society should not be Darwinistic either. In an evolved society, the weak should be just as revered as the strong. Realistically, it does not always work that way because many would argue that we are not that evolved yet as a society. OCR's demand is that if the weak cannot be revered, at least they should be protected! This position is widely held in various arenas. It is even a tenant of the martial art Tae Kwan Do that a black belt steps in and protects the weak whenever he or she sees the weak being victimized.

The school should establish a program (a strategy required by OCR) that encourages the bystander/witness to become an "up-stander" and, at a minimum, report the incident to a person in authority. It would be a step further if the witness stepped in to stop the incident, but that could be, for some, a step too far. At a minimum, the incident should be reported.

If all students adopted an up-stander posture, their school would be a lot closer to the elimination of sexual violence and sexual harassment. The school should be an area free of this abuse and discrimination.

Returning to the Shelby incident, the questions that an investigator should ask have been presented previously. Now is the time is go deeper and follow a course of action that will demonstrate a thorough investigation. Once the investigation is complete, the school is expected to render and publish a "finding" and make a fair (just) determination of next steps. The school is expected by OCR to adjudicate the micro incidents and, on a macro level, take steps to prevent similar incidents from occurring in the future.

In Shelby's case, Donald was observed committing sexual violence against Shelby by several of his peers. Often, these incidents are she said/he said cases without witnesses. In this case, however, two classmates had observed Donald, so there is no question about what happened. The two witnesses corroborated each other's account of the incident. They saw Donald grab Shelby from her back, draw her rear-end into his groin and rub up against her. They indicated that the incident lasted 10 or 15 seconds.

So, what came out of the various interviews and what happens next? The first interview was with Shelby's teacher, Ms. Coatney. She provided background on Shelby, stating that she is a nice 13-year-old girl who presents mildly with autism. She has comfortably been mainstreamed into a classroom of peers without autistic tendencies. Shelby is easier to upset than others without her condition and tends to be less able to multitask than her peers. Other then these issues, she fits in with her peers very nicely.

Regarding the micro incident with Donald Greene, she was greatly agitated and negatively affected. She was not able to articulate very well what happened to her, but she was very obvious about how she felt about it. The two witnesses gave a credible account of what happened and were upset by what they witnessed. When Ms. Coatney confronted Donald Greene, he denied that he did anything wrong—only that he was being friendly with Shelby. Ms. Coatney did not become judgmental and did not intervene other than to separate the two and address Shelby's state of distress. She knew that Donald's behavior would have to be handled at a higher level than hers and filed the report knowing that an investigation would follow.

The next interview was with Shelby and her mother. Because Shelby is a minor and because of her mental condition, it is necessary to involve her mother or father at every opportunity. This meeting, like all the other interviews, is really to gather information, rather than to give information. This meeting will be uncomfortable for the interviewer because Shelby's mother will demand to know what the school is going to do about the incident. She will be impatient and insistent that Shelby be protected and Donald Greene punished. And, she will want to know how this is going to be accomplished and will not be patient. In addition, she will not be sympathetic towards Donald Greene.

The interviewer/investigator must provide assurances that the school will do everything it can to accomplish or accommodate Shelby's mother's demands. Most parents will, quite understandably, negatively overreact, and they will be skeptical regarding the school's competence and commitment to protect their child. Unfortunately, their fears and skepticism have been warranted by many past incidents. There have been far too many incidents of children committing suicide or other calamities in the schools for parents to think otherwise.

What should the investigator/interviewer do? The first tool in the kit is interim measures. OCR requires schools to *consider* several interim measures that are at the school's disposal. They can change the student's schedule (either the alleged victim or the alleged perpetrator). They can waive or modify school policies to accommodate the alleged victim's needs, including providing more time for homework, allowing tests to be given or taken orally, late or not at all, and schools can allow for class lessons to be taken home and taught by parents for a period of time. There are many options that can be considered, and OCR regulations dictate that schools be flexible and accommodating, rather then default to their standard operating procedures (SOP). Another interim measure is to provide an adult escort for the alleged victim, so he/she is not alone between classes or out of the eyesight of an adult throughout the day. This is not easy to facilitate, but it is particularly effective as a reassurance to parents.

At the beginning of the previous paragraph, the word "consider" is emphasized. Schools are not required to provide interim measures but are required to consider them. Whether the school determines that interim measures are necessary or unnecessary, in the end, they will be judged accordingly against the outcomes of the case. Remember that this point is the very beginning of the inquiry.

The investigator/interviewer should communicate the school's commitment to Shelby's safety and well-being to her mother. She should be told what options are relative to interim measures and asked to recommend one or ones that would satisfy her concerns. She may want Donald Greene's head on a pike, but that isn't going to happen. In other words, she may want the school to take a very punitive stand with Donald Greene, but, at this point in the inquiry, Donald and his parents have not even been interviewed. Additionally, the school's position is that Shelby's safety and well-being are very important, but so is Donald's. This is not a law enforcement situation but, rather, a school, and a school is all about providing learning opportunities.

There is a distinction here between the school's interests and the interests and focus of law enforcement. This distinction is very important and must be understood. OCR regulations say that the school's investigation must proceed within the specified table. It must start within 24 hours of notice of the incident and conclude within 60 days. If there is a criminal investigation by the police, then the two investigations must proceed side by side and independently. The police investigation exists to determine if laws have been broken and to detain the perpetrators. The school's investigation exists to determine if Title IX regulations or state laws prohibiting bullying or sexual harassment and/or sexual violence have occurred. The school is charged with seeing that the victim is accommodated in some remedy and that the violation not occur again. The police investigation is not concerned with repairing the conditions for the victim, while the school's investigation is focused on that and assisting the perpetrator to grow and evolve away from repeating similarly bad behavior.

In concluding the interview with Shelby's mother, she should be assured that the interim measures agreed to will be initiated immediately and that a thorough and timely inquiry will be conducted. She should have further assurance that OCR requires that any "findings" are written and published, and that, based on those findings, appropriate action will be taken. Finally, she should be assured that she will be informed of the findings and the outcome, as that is also an OCR requirement. Shelby's mother should be told that nothing will be "swept under the rug" and that Shelby's status will be monitored for a minimum of 90 days, looking for any changes or deterioration in her academic performance, her hygiene, her connectivity to her friends, etc. The mother should be asked to help in that monitoring. If it is agreed that there is any deterioration, then further steps will be taken. When the school takes this level of interest and action, most parents will be comfortable regarding their competence and commitment.

The next interview was with Donald's homeroom teacher. She is not Ms. Coatney, who was Shelby's teacher. Donald's teacher is Ms. Briggs, a savvy teacher with a career that is decades long. Ms. Briggs pegged Donald as a kid on the edge. He was in the custody of a single mother, who was only minimally educated and worked as a waitress, making just enough money to get by. Donald had his bright spots, but there was plenty there to worry about. Like many seventh-grade boys, his interest in girls was present and far surpassed his interest in scholastic achievement. His friends did not really seem too interested in school either. Donald was not impulsive and seemed to think things out before taking action. This was something Ms. Briggs was trying to cultivate and, of course, using to steer Donald in good directions. Donald was mouthy and said things that could be unkind. Ms. Briggs admitted that Donald could go either way, meaning he could fall to the "dark side" or he could be a responsible person. She was working with him and praying for him to make good choices, hoping to be a good steward and bring out the best in him.

The next interview was with Donald Greene and his mother. Donald denied that he touched Shelby inappropriately. His version of the incident was that he did put his hands on her, but it was only in fun. His story was that he was behind her at the end of the line and only grabbed her around her waist. He did not draw her into him, and he was just keeping her from moving forward, as they were in the back of the line. Donald denied ever touching her in the past, that this was the first instance and that it was only a friendly joke—nothing more. Ms. Brown, Donald's mother made it a point to say that she was no longer married to Donald's father and since his departure, she had taken back her maiden name. She was absolutely positive that Donald had done nothing wrong and that there must be a big misunderstanding somewhere. She assured the interviewer that Donald was a good boy and that he did his homework and did well at school. His hobbies were reading, and he was on the school's archery team. His friends were all good boys, and this girl must have misread the situation as Donald was, as he indicated, just joking around with her. She also indicated that because the girl was "slow," it was easy to assume she misread the situation. She went on to suggest that most girls like the attention they get from boys.

Donald went on to say he does not really know Shelby that well. They were in line together, and it just popped into his mind to play a trick on her and that was all. He denied ever touching her or any other girl inappropriately on any other occasion. He did not think it was wrong to do what he did, but he could see that she did not appear to like what had happened. This was a bit of a surprise to him, and he said he was sorry that she did not think his trick was funny.

When asked what kind of person he was, Donald could not answer the question. His mother, Ms. Brown, was a bit incredulous and answered for her son. She said that he was a good and a smart boy. She indicated that few seventh-graders could answer such a question.

Donald was not asked about his friends because Ms. Briggs, his teacher, had told all that was needed to know about them. A note was made to circle back to her about Donald's reading and his participation on the school's archery team. Ms. Briggs indicated that Donald was not a particularly strong reader; she never saw him with a library book in his hands. After she checked the records, she said that he was not on the archery team or any other school related teams.

The next stop was to interview the two witnesses, one boy and one girl. Their parents were not called into the investigation but rather Mr. Williams, the associate principal at Longfellow Middle School, was asked to be present. He knew the two students and felt that they would be truthful and comfortable in his presence. Both students were interviewed separately, and their stories were essentially the same. One boy had more details than the other, but both could tell that Shelby was grabbed from behind and pulled into Donald's groin. The boy said that Donald was a jerk and that all he talked about was sex and girls' body parts. He also stated that Donald clearly was holding Shelby up against his private parts and that Shelby was freaking out. The incident just lasted a few seconds, but it did happen and was clearly wrong.

The girl said that she had seen Donald do this stunt before and that she made sure not to get into any line in which he would be behind her. Donald would get behind some girl and reach around and poke her or try to touch her boobs. Some girls took it as a joke, but this time Shelby did not. She said she thought she saw Donald do this to Shelby once before, but she could not be sure. Everybody knew that Shelby could not really defend herself, and since she was physically developing, other girls wondered if she would be targeted. This student told me the names of two other girls who were aware that this had happened in the past. Both students and Mr. Williams were thanked for their help. He said that he would speak to the two students the girl had mentioned and would alert the teachers to be extra vigilant.

What conclusions should be reached?

The investigation was now complete and ahead of the 60-day maximum allowed by OCR. The incident did occur, the victim was Shelby and the perpetrator was Donald. The allegation had been substantiated and now it was time for a "finding" to be rendered, a consequence to be applied and a plan implemented to ensure the situation would not be repeated. Additionally, OCR requires that the victim be protected from retaliation.

What recommended actions should be taken?

Shelby will need to be monitored for at least 90 days to make sure that she is safe from any retaliation or other improper behavior from others and to see if this incident causes any deterioration in her mental or physical state. If there were any deterioration, then an amendment to her individual education plan (IEP) would be required. Also, If Shelby had not been, prior to this incident, a 504 or IDEA student, she might now qualify for disability under one of the two laws due to this incident. The same could be true for Donald. Through the course of the investigation, it might be found that he was abused at home and therefore may now (that we know this) qualify for disability services. If any of this unfolds, steps have to be taken to qualify the child and provide for his/her needs for FAPE (free appropriate public education).

A strong conversation with Donald and his mother, Ms. Brown, will take place, and Donald will be transferred to a different school for the balance of the school year. This will represent a hardship on Donald's mother for transportation, but there will be the provision that if Donald has no further incidents (at his new school) and there is no retaliation towards Shelby, he can return to the original school the following year. As a condition of Donald remaining in the district, he will have to attend the Title IX required training program and the required perpetrator's course. He will be warned to take no action that could be considered retaliation towards Shelby. Mr. Williams, the school's associate principal, had a similar conversation with Donald's buddies. Donald is reminded that he is welcomed in the district, as long as he is behaving as a good citizen. He is on notice that his reputation and credibility is tarnished and that if there is another incident, he will be gone from the district altogether. Ms. Brown was also urged to keep a close eye on her son. She was surprised to learn that he was not on the archery team and that he had been lying to her when he told her he was away from home attending archery practice.

All interview notes were aggregated and filed. The findings and conclusions were recorded. OCR requires that the school advise the victim and perpetrator regarding the findings, the conclusions reached from the investigation and the remedies to be implemented. Not all records from the investigation need to be published. The final activity must be the steps the school district intends to take to ensure that the violation or discrimination is not repeated by the perpetrator (at a micro level), as well as the steps to be taken to ensure that the school is a safer place in the future (the macro perspective).

CHAPTER 6

CASE STUDY—UNIVERSITY

The Incident

The following case takes place in a Midwestern university's school of fine arts. There are three thousand students in the fine arts school, which means it is a big and fairly anonymous place. Like all state schools, there are financial limitations. For instance, the vocal students have to provide their own piano or musical accompaniment if they wish accompaniment for their vocal recitals and tests. The common wisdom is that the recitals and tests go better for the vocal students if they have musical accompaniment, but they are not required to have such. The typical fee for this accompaniment is $130 per event, which includes two rehearsals and the main event. The situation can put some vocal students in a financial bind.

The allegation came from college sophomore Victoria Booth, who was a vocal music major at this state conservatory. She alleged that August Baker, a Ph.D. candidate piano major at the same conservatory, had offered to provide piano accompaniment for her class vocal project. This would have not been noteworthy except that the fee for his piano accompaniment was sexual favors because Victoria could not afford to pay Mr. Baker to be her piano accompanist. This incident caused Victoria to realize how vulnerable she was due to her lack of funds. Without the piano accompaniment, her vocal presentation would be less powerful, less impressive and could probably severely impact her grade. August Baker was so forceful in his approach that Victoria became frightened for her safety. She reported the incident to me, Dr. Rodregass, the university's Title IX coordinator today, Friday October 10th.

My first steps are to determine if Title IX regulations and university policies were violated. This requires an interview with the alleged victim, Ms. Booth, to get more details regarding the incident. This is always the place to start. The alleged victim should be told that this is a confidential interview with the intention to gather facts and feelings relevant to the incident.

Ms. Booth told me that she met with Mr. Baker last Monday, October 6th (two days ago at a campus coffee shop) because she heard that he was one of the accompanists available. She said that her first impression of him was that he was handsome and friendly. The subject of money was not even raised at this first meeting. He gave her every indication that he would work with her schedule regarding her need for piano accompaniment. They agreed to meet that week on Thursday, October 9th, at one of the practice rooms at the conservatory to look over the music. The meeting took place at 8:30 p.m., and Ms. Booth arrived, only to find that she was alone. When Mr. Baker showed up, he smelled of wine but only slightly. He brought in a bottle of chilled wine and offered a glass—actually she said he offered several glasses— to Ms. Booth, and he had two glasses of wine as well. It was against the rules, but she said that she accepted the wine anyway. As he sat down at the piano, he encouraged Ms. Booth to sit next to him and share the music.

Things went smoothly for the first 45 minutes. Mr. Baker proved to be quite talented, and he played the music beautifully. Ms. Booth commented to me that she was quite taken with his talent and started to feel that his accompaniment would be a really great thing for her recital testing. Then things took a turn for the worse. Mr. Baker asked if his piano playing would work for her. She said yes and then he brought up the cost of $130 for his services. Ms. Booth was caught off guard, but she said that, in reality, she half expected the matter of money to be brought up sooner or later. She told me that she told Mr. Baker that she really liked his playing, but that she really couldn't afford his fee. By this time, Ms. Booth said that she had stood up and was standing next to the piano. She was bracing herself, leaning on the piano. While she knew she really needed him to provide her accompaniment, she just didn't have the money and did not know what to do. Mr. Baker then suggested that some other arrangements could be made. He stood up from the piano bench, and she said that she could see that he was sexually aroused. He then moved to her and embraced her, pressed his groin into her and touched her breast.

Ms. Booth began to cry at this point in the interview. I offered her a tissue and told her we could take a break. When we resumed, she indicated that she had pulled away from Mr. Baker and begun to cry. She said that he told her that she was beautiful and that he wanted to screw her. She left the practice room in tears.

I asked some follow-up questions, wondering if there were any witnesses. She had already said that they were alone in the practice room, but I was hoping that other practice rooms might have been occupied. But, unfortunately, she said that she did not hear others practicing at that time. When asked if she had told anyone else about this, she said only her best friend, Ashley Bishop, an acting student. We are now at the end of the first week. The OCR required 60-day clock, the time allowed for a thorough and timely investigation to occur, just started.

My next question focused on the depth of the feelings held by Ms. Booth. I asked her to indicate how she felt about the incident on a scale that started on the low side as "being annoyed" and progressing to the high side of feeling threatened and fearing for her safety. The intermediate steps being more of a nuisance, more of a burden or more like something that angered her. She indicated that she felt as if he would have raped her had she not been able to get away. Visibly shaking, she again started to cry. It is important to define the level of concern held by the alleged victim. Ms. Booth's emotional state is important in two ways: At the front end, there is a need to determine the interim measures to take, and at the back end to know what follow-up steps to initiate. The OCR requires schools to provide whatever services are necessary and at the school's expense.

I finished taking her statement and determined that the incident did constitute a violation of both campus policy and Title IX. The incident specifically can be referred to, at a minimum, as sexual harassment. It could also be viewed as sexual violence and, perhaps, attempted sexual battery.

I asked Ms. Booth to consider what steps (interim measures) the university might take to assist her, and she asked about the options available. I indicated that we could modify her schedule, we could postpone her vocal tests and/or we could even provide an escort so that she would not be alone and vulnerable. She seemed relieved that I was willing to take steps to protect her and asked for a day or two to think things over. In response to her request, I notified her teachers that she would not be attending class for the next day or so.

Accessing school records to look up Ms. Victoria Booth and Mr. August Baker was the next step. There was little in Ms. Booth's record because she had only been enrolled for three semesters. She had good grades and was active in campus activities—not a sorority member but lived on campus in the dorms. She seemed like a well-adjusted student matriculating normally. I checked her schedule with the intention of comparing it to that of Mr. Baker's schedule, hoping that they did not overlap.

Mr. Baker had been on campus for three years as a doctoral level graduate student majoring in piano at the conservatory. Checking his schedule, I found one point on each Tuesday and Thursday that he could easily run into Ms. Booth at the conservatory. Not good. Also noting the faculty person who works with Mr. Baker, I organized interviews with him.

The very next interview after the alleged victim is always the alleged perpetrator. I could have done more reconnaissance on Mr. Baker by interviewing the various faculty members who supervise his studies, but I decided to address him first. They and their opinions could wait a bit.

I called Mr. Baker in for an interview and advised him of the allegation made by Ms. Booth against him. He was very cool and proclaimed complete ignorance and innocence and acknowledged that he had not known Ms. Booth prior to this week. But, as a result of her call to him, they met and discussed his helping her by providing piano accompaniment. He admitted to meeting her at the practice room and demonstrating his capabilities to assist her but denied bringing wine into the building and denied any touching or anything inappropriate. Mr. Baker said that when he brought up his fee for providing the piano accompaniment, she told him she could not pay, so he ended the session and left. He presented the situation as a simple business transaction, which she could not afford. And, he presented himself as professional and could not understand why she would make such an allegation. Baffling. Mr. Baker, soon to be Dr. Baker and promising piano virtuoso, was "above it all" in his demeanor.

Letting him know that I would probably have more questions for him later, I thanked him for coming in to speak with me. I told him that it was strictly routine, but I had to warn him to take no action that might be considered controversial and to take no action that might be considered retaliation. He simply smirked and left my office.

I had a thought and called Ms. Booth on the phone. When she answered, I asked her about the bottle of chilled wine she said Mr. Baker brought with him into the practice room. Did she remember where he placed the bottle in the room after he poured their drinks? She thought for a minute and said that he placed the bottle on the top of the piano. Which, she remembered, would probably have left a stain or ring on the piano because the bottle was sweating. At the time, she thought it was odd that he would treat the instrument that thoughtlessly. After she recalled the number of the practice room for me, I took the opportunity to ask her if she was ready to come back to school and what interim measures she felt she needed. We agreed to meet later that day. I "hotfooted" over to the conservatory and up to the practice room, where I proceeded to the room Ms. Booth had indicated and, sure enough, there was a condensation ring on the lid of the piano that resembled one from a chilled bottle.

Next, I went to the office and inquired about the way students reserve practice rooms. The secretary told me about the log-on reservation process and found the notation in the log where August Baker had reserved that room. I asked if that room had been used since the Baker reservation, and she said yes by one student and told me the student's name and her contact information. In passing, I asked the secretary if she knew a student named August Baker, and she made a face that looked like she had just been asked to do something extremely unpleasant. She indicated that he was known to her, and most people, as a narcissistic jerk. He had plenty of talent on the piano, but his people skills were all but nonexistent. I thanked her and made my notes.

Contacting the student who had reserved the same practice room after Mr. Baker, I asked her if she had noticed a bottle ring stain on the lid of the piano when she was practicing. Confirming that she had, she said that she thought it was pretty unusual to see such neglect and contempt paid to the piano. This did not prove much except that it revealed a lie told to me by Mr. Baker—we were getting places.

I then met with Ms. Booth, and she thanked me and the university for being so considerate and stated that she was ready to resume her classes but had some fear about running into the pianist. She did not know if he would pursue her, but she did take his comments seriously. Asking if my offer to have her escorted around campus were still on the table, I assured her that it was and could have someone available the following day. We agreed to meet in the morning at my office where I would introduce her to Justin, a physical therapy major with a black belt in Te KwanDo, who had agreed to go into "secret service" mode for this. I figured that a week or two at the most would be needed, and he had indicated that he could line up some backup, and Ms. Booth would be covered to and from the dorms and between classes. He also said he was looking forward to hearing her sing. Although, I suspected that he and his buddies were not concerned about a piano grad student—that was for sure. Great.

Next in the interview process would be character witnesses for both the alleged victim and the alleged perpetrator. The basic question is, "Is it in the character of the person to do what is being alleged?" So, would the alleged victim, Ms. Booth, lie about what happened? Could or would the alleged perpetrator do what Ms. Booth said happened? Since there were no actual witnesses to the incident, it often comes down to character, and the reputation of the participants will be called into the investigation. The behavioral premise is that the best predictor of future performance or behavior is past performance or behavior. The secretary at the conservatory had already given me a character reference on Mr.

Baker, when she had a visceral reaction to the mention of his name. Let's see where this goes.

I ran down three faculty members who teach Victoria Booth. Their impressions were roughly the same, a very nice young lady with a reasonably bright talent for vocal music. One faculty member described her as very good-looking and rather shy about her looks. She was no Barbara Streisand musically, but she was a hard worker with guts and heart. The consensus was that she was honest and demonstrated integrity, was reliable and followed through on commitments. She was not prone to "diva" antics. In fact, it was the opposite—very "down-to-earth." I was coming to the conclusion that she was not a liar, and it was not in her character to exaggerate charges or to exaggerate her allegation against Mr. Baker.

I interviewed her best friend, Ms. Ashley Bishop, who I found to be a bit different from Victoria Booth. A lot different actually. She was loud, tall and imposing. Also a student, she was in the fine arts program but in the acting department. Having met in the dorms, she and Ms. Booth had been friends since the last year. And, she confided in me that she and Ms. Booth were twins. There was a big laugh, and a wink from Ms. Bishop—clearly a budding actor. We got down to the business at hand, and she readily acknowledged that Victoria was freaked by what had happened with the "asshole," her words to describe the pianist. She would not use Mr. Baker's name, but she shared the account of what she had been told by Ms. Booth. It was consistent with what Ms. Booth had told me just a few days ago. Ms. Bishop added that she wished someone who was sexually aroused would rub up against her! When you interview, you just never know what you will get.

Now about two weeks into the investigation, I have interviews scheduled with two of Mr. Baker's faculty—one teacher in the piano program and his faculty advisor. The piano faculty member was aloof and walked like a stork. He was perhaps 6' 4" and drew out his words with an air of sophistication and pomp, as he described Mr. Baker as an immense talent on the piano. Mr. Baker would be a great musical presence throughout the entire world one day. He would be a great reflection of the conservatory and so on. Blah, blah, blah.

This teacher had no clue about Mr. Baker's interpersonal side and seemed annoyed at the very notion of something as trivial as Mr. Baker's people skills was being brought up at all. When I asked him if he thought it was in Mr. Baker's character to bring wine into the practice room, even though it was against the rules to have alcohol on campus, he just smiled and said that some rules are silly and unimportant. What was important was to develop one's talent and that is exactly what Mr. Baker was doing. He advised me to leave Mr. Baker alone so that he could pursue his studies. He was aware of Mr. Baker acting as a vocal student accompanist and stated that it was a way to supplement his student's income—there was nothing wrong with it. Asked if he saw an opportunity in the practice to take advantage of other students who needed the accompanist but couldn't pay for it, he considered the question and simply raised his eyebrows. No answer was given, and I was dismissed with a statement that he had a student who was scheduled.

My next interview was with Mr. Baker's faculty advisor. Dr. Danforth gave the impression of an aging aristocrat. He had a neat, grey Van Dyke beard, snappy tie and wore a sport coat with patches on the elbows. He was a bit stodgy, perhaps 1940's, but not too much so. Dr. Danforth said that he knew August Baker pretty well and that Mr. Baker was in his last semester of his doctoral work. He had great talent at the keyboard but seemed to regard people as tools to use and then disregard. When I sought explanation, he gave me an example of how Mr. Baker demanded that the piano tuner be called in at the last possible minute prior to using it to test it for him. The faculty tester informed Dr. Danforth that the piano was only very slightly out of tune but; nonetheless, it was not acceptable to Mr. Baker. Having left other work to retune the "not so out of tune" piano that Baker was to play, Baker apparently rudely dismissed him once it reached his satisfaction. No thanks and no appreciation expressed or offered, a shameful display of narcissism. While Dr. Danforth acknowledged Baker's talent on the piano and the expectation that his talent would take him to high places, he also seemed to regret that Baker lacked any sort of compassion for other people.

I asked Dr. Danforth if he were aware of the practice of the vocal majors having to personally pay for piano accompaniment. He stated that he was aware of the practice. He did acknowledge that it was a way for students like Baker to supplement their income but on the backs of the other students and seemed to regret the zero sum in the equation. I asked him if he knew, or could find out, if Mr. Baker performed this service for others, and if he could, to please get me their contact information. He ended by saying he would try to call me in a few days; I thanked him and pushed off.

I went back to the vocal department at the conservatory and inquired about the practice of the vocal students paying personally for their accompaniment, learning that the practice had been in place for a few years. It was not a perfect solution they said but one necessitated by the lack of university funds.

After obtaining a list of the vocal students who had used piano accompanists in the recent past, I located three current students from the list and even managed to run down a student that had graduated the previous year from the vocal program. Two of them had had the occasion to use Mr. Baker's services, so I scheduled face-to-face interviews with the two who were familiar with Mr. Baker and the other one granted me a phone interview.

The phone interview with the one that used another piano accompanist was critical of the necessity to use her own funds for such an important service. She reiterated that having piano accompaniment was essential, not just a nicety and thought it was shameful that the school did not provide the service as part of the regular tuition. She said that it was common practice for the sweet, young vocalists to be taken advantage of by the piano students. Asking her to explain what she meant by that, her tone suggested I was a stupid child. "The vocal students learn quickly what they must do —they must do it on their backs," she said and then hung up on me.

The other two students agreed to meet me. One was a girl who was relatively unattractive compared to Ms. Booth who said that working with Mr. Baker was rather uncomfortable. He was condescending to her and barely treated her with any courtesy at all, considering she paid him a lot of money. Admitting that his piano talent was obvious and that he added enormously to her vocal presentation, she said she would use him again but would not like the experience much.

The other student, Ms. Bella Ravin, was very attractive. She was petite and had a kind of "wow" power in her look and persona. She remembered hiring Baker and described him "undressing her with his eyes." He had met with her and discussed his providing her with piano accompaniment but did not mention money until they got to the practice room. After working on the music for a while, he brought up his fee. She said he looked genuinely disappointed when she agreed to pay his fee and hinted that he would be willing to work something out with her if she had trouble coming up with the money. Ms. Ravin said that she assured him that the money was not a problem, but it was clear to her that he was willing to trade his fee for sex if she were interested. In conclusion, she said that she was really glad that her parents were able to come up with the extra cash for her accompaniment, as this Baker character had looked at her like she was slice of meat.

I was now finished with my investigation. My finding is that the allegation by Ms. Victoria Booth against Mr. August Baker is substantiated. My obligation now is to render a formal finding and remedy. This must be provided to the parties. My obligation to follow the OCR's regulations includes completing my investigation in 60 days or less, considering and installing appropriate interim measures, reaching a conclusion that attempts to mitigate the harm done to both the victim and to the institution (other students) and then communicate that remedy to both parties. The final obligation is to monitor the victim for a period of 90 days or more to ensure that (in this case) she does not suffer any deterioration in her grades or personally as a result of the incident.

So why did I substantiate the allegation? There were no actual witnesses and no smoking gun, but there was enough discovered to allow me to render a finding against Mr. Baker.

I will break it down as follows:

Motive

- A pattern in Mr. Baker's motis operandi (his MO). Ms. Bella Ravin's account of what happened to her was similar enough to what happened to Ms. Victoria Booth.
- The secretary's account of Mr. Baker's lack of empathy toward her.
- The faculty advisor's (Dr. Danforth) personal account and the incident with the piano tuner demonstrated Mr. Baker's character.
- The attitude demonstrated by Mr. Baker's piano faculty advisor (Dr. Stork), suggesting that the interpersonal dimension is unimportant.
- The lie about the wine consumption.

Opportunity

The conservatory's policy of requiring the vocal majors to pay for the accompaniment personally places those students with financial limitations into a compromising situation with the piano accompanists.

So how does the university assure a remedy for the micro-incident victim (Ms. Booth) and how does the university assure that the problem is solved on a macro level? I went to my boss, the university provost, who is really the COO (chief operating officer) of the university and apprised him regarding the micro and macro of the case. Focusing on Mr. Baker, I argued that we permanently expel him. By getting him off campus, he would not be in any position to prey on any future vocal students. Focusing on the macro, I recommended that the university begin to provide the piano accompaniment and not place that financial burden on the vocal students.

The provost urged me to moderate my recommendation regarding expelling Mr. Baker. Such a move would effectively render it impossible for him to finish his doctorate there or anywhere else, as no other school would take him under these circumstances. This would, in the provost's opinion, render an undo hardship on Mr. Baker. He suggested that we eject Mr. Baker out of the program for one academic year and then allow him to petition to return on a probationary status to finish his advanced degree in piano. Conditions would be placed on his return, including being required to take the OCR required perpetrator's course of training, to submit to professional counseling with the school having access to those records and, perhaps, other requirements.

Regarding the recommendation to eliminate the requirement for individuals to pay for piano accompaniment on their own, he approved but came up with a plan to establish a private fund provided by donors so the university directly did not need to heft those costs. The provost approved the completions of my findings, and I proceeded to communicate with the dean of the conservatory about Mr. Baker's punishment. The dean and I would individually deliver the news to both the victim, vindicating her, and to the perpetrator, advising him of his fate and ordering him to vacate the campus.

The way the OCR requires the notification process, the victim is notified orally and in writing as to the outcome of the investigation. The victim is told the consequences imposed on the perpetrator and what steps the school is to take regarding the victim's follow-up support. The perpetrator is told nothing of what support the victim receives, only what is going to happen to the perpetrator. This is also done in writing and orally.

I asked Ms. Booth to be sure to let me know if she needed anything in the way of assistance from the university and that we would be watching her for at least 90 days. Regarding Mr. Baker, we advised him to take no steps to make any contact with Ms. Booth, as there would be zero tolerance on our part for any behavior that suggested retaliation. He could return to campus in a year and complete his degree. We let him know we would be watching him. Further, I advised that if there were any future complaints about him sexually harassing other students, he would be expelled on the spot.

Ms. Booth was appreciative and proceeded with her vocal education. Mr. Baker left campus for parts unknown. A fund was established called Victoria's Scholarship, and the policy requiring vocal majors personally pay for their accompaniment was abolished. I later found out that the students developed their own name for the scholarship. Instead of referring to it as Victoria's Scholarship, they referred to the recipients as Booth Babes!

CHAPTER 7

CASE STUDY—EIGHTH GRADE

Incident and Investigation

It started sometime in March of 2015. Eighth-grader Allison Jones was in the hallway going from one class to another, and someone came up behind her and snapped her bra strap. That happened two, maybe three times, and in each incident, by the time she turned around to see who was doing this (let's just say because of the congestion in the hallway), the perpetrator was not obvious. Her bustline was growing, and the boys clearly were taking notice. She was not dressing in a provocative way or trying to bring attention to her blooming femininity. The next incident occurred when a boy (again in the hallway between classes) reached out and groped her chest. This time, she could identify him, although she did not know his name and that he was with another boy. After she was inappropriately touched, Allison observed that the boys laughed, and she was left her in the hallway in a shocked state of mind. By the end of the day, she decided to tell her mother.

The next morning, her mother called the school and spoke with the principal, Ms. Jane Kitchin, insisting that Ms. Kitchin meet with her immediately. Later that day, Allison and her mother met with the principal, and Allison relayed the four incidents. The principal listened and assured Ms. Jones that the matter would be investigated. Ms. Jones asked what was going to be done to ensure that the incidents stop and not be repeated. Ms. Kitchin assured both Allison and Ms. Jones that she would assign someone to escort Allison to and from classes for the next few days and that the word would get out that Allison was being watched. The next day, and for about a week thereafter, a teacher was assigned to walk with Allison as she changed classes.

The district's Title IX coordinator assigned a trained investigator to conduct an examination of Allison's allegations. The day after the meeting with the principal, Allison's homeroom teacher, Ms. Williams, interviewed Allison and completed the following incident report:

On Tuesday, April 8, 2015, eighth-grader Allison Jones at Indian Hills Middle School was between classes near her locker and just outside room 208 at approximately 1:35 p.m. She was walking north to her sixth-period math class. The hallway was congested with many students traveling to their next classes when she felt a person's hand squeeze her right breast. She slapped the hand away and turned to see a boy in proximity close enough to have been the perpetrator. He was laughing, and he had a friend with whom he was obviously communicating. Allison did not know the name of this student but described him as Caucasian and about 5'5" with blond hair and wearing a bright red shirt that had the name of a soft drink on the front. The other boy was much taller than the first, perhaps 5'9" and African American. According to Allison, when he made eye contact with Allison, his face turned "menacing." She did not know this student's name either. In addition, Allison relayed that there had been two or three other incidences over the past month where her bra strap had been snapped by an unknown person or persons while she was in the hallway between classes. Regarding potential witnesses, there were many students in the hallway when the incident occurred according to Allison, but there was just one student that she knew by name, Robert Wilson.

Ms. Williams assured Allison that she would be contacted within 24 hours by the district's investigator, and the full inquiry would begin. A phone call to Allison's mother was also placed.

The very next morning, Ms. Roberta Lawrence, a Title IX investigator for the district, contacted Allison and asked her to meet at exactly 1:15 outside of room 208. She assured Allison that she would square things with Allison's teachers if she missed her class. When they met, Ms.

Lawrence introduced herself and briefly reviewed the details contained in the report filed by Ms. Williams, and Allison acknowledged that the details were accurate. Ms. Lawrence indicated that they were going to watch the "goings on" in the hallway, and if Allison spotted either of the two students allegedly involved in the incident, she should point them out to her.

Shortly, Allison identified the African American student, but the actual (alleged) perpetrator was not. The identified student was called over and required to show his student ID to Ms. Lawrence. Once the formal ID was completed and the name (Raymond Hilliard) was secured, he was advised by Ms. Lawrence that he could go on to class but that he could expect to be called for an interview within a few days. He was warned to take no action that could be considered provocative or retaliatory toward Allison or things could go very badly for him.

The following is the Report of Findings filed by Ms. Lawrence after she completed her investigation:

Memo

To: Title IX File

Fr: Ms. Roberta Lawrence, Title IX investigator, XYZ School District

Date: dd/mm/year

RE: Investigation 02166 involving complainant Allison Jones

Confidential Executive Summary:

On Thursday April 10, 2015, I was advised that a Title IX complaint was filed by Indian Hills Middle School eighth-grader Allison Jones. She and her mother met with Indian Hills Middle School Principal Ms. Kitchen on April 9, 2015, who assigned Allison Jones' homeroom teacher, Ms. Williams, to interview Allison and complete the district's Title IX complaint form (see attached). The allegation is that on Tuesday, April 8, 2015, at approximately 1:35 p.m., Allison was groped by another student while navigating the school hallway on her way to her sixth-hour math class. The incident lasted only a few seconds. Allison Jones saw an arm reach around from behind her and felt a hand squeeze her right breast. It was described by Allison as a deliberate motion of the arm and squeeze of the hand and not an accidental touch or brush. Allison was wearing a pink Oxford-type blouse that buttoned down the front, and the perpetrator got his fingers between the buttons of the blouse and made contact with the bra covering Allison's right breast. The contact only occurred or lasted for a second, as Allison instinctively slapped the hand away. After the contact, Allison turned around to see a male student, unknown to her, who appeared to be the perpetrator. He was laughing and communicating with another unknown male student. Allison described these two unknown male students in some detail. She said they turned and left immediately after the incident was perpetrated. Allison did not report the alleged incident until the following day, when she and her mother met with Principal Kitchin.

Principal Kitchin initiated the interim measure of having Allison escorted between all classes by an adult faculty member. That interim measure was in place for eight school days until April 19, 2015, when Allison acknowledged that she was comfortable enough to travel between classes unescorted after that time.

The formal investigation began with a meeting with Allison on April 10, 2015. At that time, she was asked to meet the investigator, Ms. Lawrence, at the exact location of the alleged incident. Ms. Lawrence met her ahead of the exact time of the alleged incident to introduce herself and to go over the data contained in the initial complaint report. After receiving clarification of some of the details of the alleged incident, both observed the scene in order to attempt to identify the alleged perpetrator and any witness who might exist. Allison was not able to identify the alleged perpetrator but was able to identify the African American student who appeared to be friends with the alleged perpetrator. Confronting him, Ms. Lawrence obtained his student ID. He was Raymond Hilliard, a ninth-grader at Indian Hills Middle School, and she advised him to be prepared to be interviewed. He was further advised and warned to take no steps that could be considered provocative or retaliatory in nature. Ms. Lawrence interviewed Allison in detail and then interviewed Raymond Hilliard. Eventually, it came out that Rodney Oldfield was the student who had groped Allison. Raymond Hilliard did not admit that Rodney Oldfield groped Allison. Hilliard did admit that he and Rodney were there but that he did not see Rodney actually touch Allison. Rodney Oldfield also denied that he groped Allison.

Ms. Lawrence then interviewed another student, Sean McKinna, a ninth-grader at the school, who had come forward and stated that he had witnessed the alleged incident. His witness was convincing, and his additional statements, along with those of some of the teachers she had interviewed, helped Ms. Lawrence come to her final conclusion. The actual groping incident had been preceded by at least two incidents where Allison had had her bra strap "snapped" while navigating the school hallways between classes. These incidents and the culminating groping incident had caused Allison to be distracted and distressed, as she worried about her safety and grew humiliated by the occurrences. Ms. Lawrence also interviewed several of the teachers of Allison Jones, Rodney Oldfield, Sean McKinna and Raymond Hilliard and obtained the teachers' perspectives regarding the character of each student. All students were invited to call for a hearing, to be represented by legal council and even call witnesses if they wished. All declined in writing.

After a thorough investigation of the allegation, the investigator determined that the allegation was substantiated as true and that the incident rose to the level of a Title IX incident because it met the definition of a hostile sexual environment. Ms. Lawrence's recommendation, after discussions with Mr. Larry Harms, the district's Title IX coordinator, was that Rodney Oldfield be suspended for 10 days. As an accomplice, Raymond Hilliard should be suspended for three days. Each of these students should be warned that any further incidents or any retaliation toward Allison Jones would result in their expulsion from Indian Hills Middle School or from the district. He further recommended that Allison Jones be followed for a period of six months to ensure that she was not further exposed to a hostile sexual environment and that no drop in her academic or social development would occur.

The Interview Process

Note: In order to provide a detailed and accurate example of the interview process from start to finish, the initial interviews with Allison and her mother must be included. At times, they will contain the same information given previously in the chapter.

Ms. Lawrence's first interview was with Allison Jones on April 12, 2015, with her mother, Ms. Jones, present. Ms. Lawrence advised that this was a confidential Title IX investigation and asked Allison to keep the information they talked about confidential. Allison agreed and proceeded to share the following information:

It started in March of 2015. She was in the hallway going from one class to another class, and someone would come up behind her and snap her bra strap. This happened two, maybe three times, and, in each incidence, by the time she turned around to see who was doing this and because of the congestion in the hallway, it was not obvious or apparent to her just who the perpetrator might have been. She indicated that she dressed "normally" and not in a way that might suggest or communicate sexuality. The fourth incident occurred when a boy (again in the hallway between classes) reached out and groped her chest. This time she could identify a perpetrator, although she did not know his name. He was with another boy. After she was inappropriately touched, she observed that they laughed and then left her in the hallway in a shocked state of mind. By the end of the day, she had decided to tell her mother about the incident. Allison indicated that the bra strap snapping incidents had occurred at different times of the day and in different locations. She was not sure about the specific times or locations but adamant that they did occur.

The interview now focused on the groping incident on April 8, 2015. The incident occurred at approximately 1:35 p.m. and approximately in front of room 208, as Allison was on her way to her sixth-hour math class. The incident lasted only a few seconds. Allison saw an arm reach around from behind her and felt a hand squeeze her right breast. It was described by her, as a deliberate motion of the arm and squeeze of the hand and not an accidental touch or brush. Allison was wearing an oxford-type blouse that buttoned down the front, and the perpetrator got his fingers between the buttons of the blouse and made contact with the bra covering her right breast. The contact only occurred or lasted for a second, as Allison instinctively slapped the hand away.

After she slapped his hand away, Allison turned to see a boy close enough to have been the perpetrator. He was laughing, and he had a friend with whom he was obviously communicating. Allison did not know the names of either of these students but described the one she thought had touched her as a Caucasian boy about 5'5" with blond hair and wearing a bright red shirt with the name of a soft drink on the front. The other boy was much taller than the first, perhaps 5'9" and African American. When he, the African American student, made eye contact with Allison, his face turned "menacing," according to her. Allison did not know this student's name either. Another student, Robert Wilson, was identified by Allison as present, but Allison did not think he had any part in the incident.

After the incident on April 8th, Indian Hills Middle School Principal Jane Kitchin met with Allison and her mother (on April 9th), learned of the incident and initiated the interim protective measure of having Allison escorted between classes by a faculty or staff member for eight school days after the groping incident. Allison stated that she was comforted by the presence of her escort. She also indicated during Ms. Lawrence's interview that she was now nervous and distracted from her studies. She was worried about what might happen to her next. Her mother, Ms. Jones, was present during this interview and was also agitated by the incident, pointing out that Allison was not prone to exaggeration nor would she bear false witness. Ms. Jones stated that she wanted her daughter to be protected, and she wanted things to be "fixed."

Allison was asked to describe her feelings about the groping incident, as well as her feelings about the bra-snapping incidents. She indicated that, at first, she was annoyed but then it began to feel "freaky" to her. She wondered and worried if she were being targeted. She did not tell her mother about these bra-snapping incidents, but she had become concerned. Allison expressed that she became frustrated and was mad at herself because she could not tell who was doing this to her. Ms. Jones expressed her dismay with her daughter for not saying anything to her about the incidents. Allison further expressed that she was self-conscience about her breasts growing and becoming obvious. Ms. Jones indicated that Allison was not "boy crazy" in any way based on Allison's conversations at home. When Ms. Lawrence asked Allison how she felt now, Allison began to cry.

Allison and her mother were assured that the incident would be investigated thoroughly and in a timely manner and that the investigation would be professional and impartial. Ms. Lawrence asked them to be patient for a few days. Additionally, she asked Allison to report it immediately if she experienced anything that she considered to be inappropriate, provocative or retaliatory as the district would not tolerate anything of that sort. Both Allison and her mother were told that they had the right to be represented by legal council or someone other than a lawyer; they had the right to call for a hearing and could present witness if they wished. They declined all of these rights for the moment. Allison was visibly concerned about a hearing. The interview lasted 80 minutes.

Ms. Lawrence's next interview was April 13, 2015 with Raymond Hilliard, the ninth-grade student Allison had identified as the student who appeared to be with the student who had groped her. Raymond was accompanied by his guardian and grandmother, Ms. Doris Silver. He was advised that this was a confidential Title IX matter and asked to keep the information discussed confidential, and he agreed. Raymond was further advised that this was an impartial investigation of an alleged incident and also had the definitions of impartial and alleged explained to him. He was then asked if he understood. He said he did, and Ms. Lawrence proceeded. Ms. Silver said that she did not understand why Raymond was being questioned. She asked if he was being accused of something and by what authority Ms. Lawrence was conducting the investigation. After Ms. Lawrence explained it to her and when she said she understood, they proceeded.

Ms. Lawrence told Raymond that it was alleged by Allison Jones that he seemed to be with another student who inappropriately touched Allison's chest. Raymond snickered and was corrected by Ms. Silver, who reminded him that this was a serious matter. Ms. Lawrence thanked Ms. Silver and also told Raymond that the matter was serious and that if the incident did occur, the full weight of the guilt could fall on him. After that, he got serious. It was further explained that if the incident did occur, that she, Ms. Lawrence, intended to get to "the bottom of it." When asked if he ever touched Allison while they were in the hallway between classes, he denied ever touching her or even knowing her. And, when asked if he were with anyone who touched Allison while they were in the hallway between classes, he denied that as well. Ms. Lawrence then asked him if he frequented that particular hallway while between classes. He acknowledged that he did. When Ms. Lawrence asked Raymond if he knew Allison, Ms. Silver reminded her that Raymond had already said he did not know her. Raymond was asked if he had ever noticed Allison while at school, and he admitted that he had seen her "around" school. Asked what it was about Allison that had caused him to notice her, he admitted that she was good looking and that is what caused him to take notice of her.

In response to who his friends were at school, Raymond gave five names, which Ms. Lawrence recorded in her notes, including noting two of the names Raymond said were his best friends. It was a forceful conversation, but Raymond assured Ms. Lawrence that neither he nor any of his friends did anything to Allison. She told him that if that turned out not to be true, there would be severe consequences for him. Further, he was told that neither he nor his friends should take any action that might be considered provocative or retaliatory toward Allison, and the definition of those words was explained. He said he understood and would comply with those orders. The interview lasted 50 minutes.

The next interview, April 13, 2015 was with Robert Wilson an eighth-grader at the school. Allison had identified him as being present when the alleged groping incident occurred. Robert and his father met with Ms. Lawrence. They were enjoined to confidentiality, and it was explained that Robert had been identified by Allison as being present in the hallway, but not a participant in the incident. Robert said that he was just on his way to his Western Civ. class and did not see anything. He knew Allison, but that was all. He did say that he had heard a rumor that some older boys in the school were doing "stuff" to girls in the hallways, but he did not know what "stuff" they were doing. After questioning Robert thoroughly, Ms. Lawrence came away convinced that he knew nothing relevant to the incident. The interview lasted 16 minute

Principal Kitchin advised Ms. Lawrence that a ninth grade student, Sean McKinna, had come to the office and said that he had seen the incident with Allison. Ms. Lawrence made an appointment with Sean and his father.

On April 14, 2015, she met with Sean and his father, Mr. McKinna. Sean's father told Ms. Lawrence that his son had told him he did see what happened and that Sean wanted to do the "right thing" and tell the investigator about it. He was strong in his opinion but was concerned for Sean's safety, as being a bystander and a whistle blower had consequences. Sean was thanked for being an "up-stander," not just a bystander and told that showing concern for his fellow students was a good thing and even an important thing. Ms. Lawrence indicated that being an "up-stander" was part of being a good person and a big part of making Indian Hills Middle School a good place to learn and grow up.

Sean was asked what he saw on April 8, 2015 at about 1:35 p.m. He said that he was in the hallway going to his next class, and he saw two boys, a "white kid named Rod 'something'" and a "black kid named Ray 'something'" come up behind this girl and touch her chest. When asked to be specific, he said that the white kid came up behind the girl and grabbed her boob. When asked which breast was touched, he said the right one and, when questioned, was able to relate that the shirt the girl had been wearing was pink and a button-down style. Continuing, Ms. Lawrence asked him if he knew the girl, and he said no but that he had noticed her before because she was really cute, and she had a great body. Sean was blushing and obviously embarrassed by the specifics he was describing.

Then Sean was asked to talk about the boy, Rod "something." Sean said that this boy was in his math class, as was the student whose name was Hilliard. He said that they were pretty tight together and always talking about the girls and their bodies and what they would like to do with them. It made Sean even more uncomfortable, but Ms. Lawrence asked him to continue. Sean added that Rod and Ray were friends with other guys and girls, and sex was all they talked about.

Sean was asked if he had heard about a game or activity where the boys came up behind girls and snapped their bra straps. Smiling meekly, he said that it was going on in the school. He did not think it was an organized game, but he knew it was something that did happen regularly. Boys, he said, talked about it a lot. He did not want to say who he had heard discussing it.

After thanking Sean, Ms. Lawrence told him that if he experienced any problems with these or other kids at school, to get to her or Ms. Kitchin immediately. After Sean said he would, he and his father left. The interview lasted for 33 minutes. Ms. Lawrence went to the class roster and identified Rod "somebody" as Rodney Oldfield.

The interview with Rodney Oldfield was next. On April 16, 2015, Ms. Lawrence asked Rodney and his mother, Ms. Oldfield, to meet with her. She began the interview with an explanation that this was a confidential Title IX investigation and enjoined Rodney to confidentiality. Ms. Oldfield said nothing. When Ms. Lawrence asked Rodney if he knew Allison Jones, an eighth-grade student at Indian Hills Middle School, he denied knowing her. In answer to whether he used the hallway in front of room 208 to get to and from classes, he said that he did. Rodney was defensive and a bit cocky in his demeanor. Shown a picture of Allison, he was again asked if he knew her and, again, he denied it.

Continuing, Ms. Lawrence asked him what he thought of Allison from her picture, and he said that she looked "hot." He was questioned extensively and kept to his story of denial and innocence in the matter. Rodney was asked if he were aware of the practice of boys in the school coming up behind girls and snapping their bra straps. He said he was aware of some boys doing that, and it was kind of a game the upperclassmen played on the younger girls. Ms. Lawrence asked him if he participated and if he approved of such behavior. He denied participating but that he didn't see the harm. Next, Ms. Oldfield was then asked if she saw the harm, to which she responded that it wasn't right, and the older boys should not do such a thing. She agreed to say this to Rodney, and his expression with his mother was "So what!" Now Ms. Lawrence asked Rodney if he thought groping girls was appropriate, and he said that it probably was not, clarifying that it was not appropriate "in school."

He made it clear that it might be appropriate in other situations. Ms. Lawrence thanked Ms. Oldfield and Rodney for their time and advised Rodney not to do or say anything to Allison or anyone else who might, in any way, be considered provocative or retaliatory. Rodney's response was noncommittal. The interview lasted 65 minutes.

Continuing the investigative phase of the incident, the next interview took place on April 16, 2015 with Ms. Williams, who was Allison's homeroom teacher. Ms. Lawrence explained the Title IX investigation she was undertaking and asked her to describe Allison. Ms. Williams stated that Allison was a relatively quiet girl who had a few friends and was a well-adjusted, good student. Then Ms. Lawrence asked her to comment about Allison's character and if it were like her to make things up or to be overly dramatic about things going on in her life. Ms. Williams described Allison to be someone who was reliable and honest, adding that Allison had a "good head on her shoulders" and came from a good family. Ms. Williams was thanked and asked to watch Allison for the next several weeks and months to determine if there were any changes for the worse. If so, she was to report those changes immediately, and she agreed. The interview lasted 12 minutes.

The next-to-last interview took place on April 16, 2015 with Dominic Riley, the homeroom teacher for Sean McKinna. After briefly explaining the Title IX investigation she was undertaking, Ms. Lawrence asked him to describe Sean. He did so, describing Sean as a strong-willed boy, good with his schoolwork and with solid parental involvement in his life. Mr. Williams was asked to comment on Sean's character—if it were in Sean's character to make things up or to be overly dramatic about things going on in his life. Mr. Riley described Sean to be someone reliable, honest and dependable. He had made friends with other "good kids," and he was glad to have Sean in his class. The interview lasted 15 minutes.

The final interview on April 17, 2015 involved Reggie Woodson, the homeroom teacher for Rodney Oldfield and Raymond Hilliard. Ms. Lawrence briefly explained the Title IX investigation and asked him to comment on the character and his experience with Rodney and Raymond. He said that the two were clearly close friends and that their behavior was a bit "on the crude side." All they talked about were girls; they were aggressive, competitive and not great students academically. Mr. Woodson relayed an incident in which the two clearly had erections and showed that fact off to a girl in the class. He said that when he told them to "knock it off," they laughed wildly and had clearly loved embarrassing the girl. Mr. Woodson said that he probably should have disciplined them, but he did not. The interview lasted 20 minutes.

Conclusion

Ms. Lawrence's conclusion was that, regardless of Rodney Oldfield's denials, there were enough findings to determine that the allegation against him was substantiated and found to be true. She also concluded that the statements made by Raymond Hilliard were also false and that the two students failed to be honest and failed to show any contrition related to the incident of groping Allison. In fact, in her opinion, the opposite appeared to be displayed.

It was further her feeling that the matter was significant and should be dealt with severely. Allison Jones had been exposed to a hostile sexual environment. The district's policy definition is the following: A hostile sexual environment exists when, "conduct of a sexual nature is sufficiently severe, persistent, or pervasive so as to limit a student's ability to participate in or benefit from the education program, or to create a hostile or abusive environment." It can't be emphasized enough that this cannot be "banter" but, rather, persistent or pervasive misconduct that has the effect of limiting the student's ability to participate in or benefit from the educational program offered by the school.

Allison Jones had been sexually harassed, and in Ms. Lawrence's opinion, Rodney Oldfield and Raymond Hilliard had lied about their involvement. No direct tie could be made that they participated in the snapping of Allison's bra strap, but it was egregious enough that she had been groped.

The recommendation was that Rodney Oldfield be suspended for a period of 10 school days and be required to take the Title IX perpetrator's course. He should be sternly warned that he will be subject to further disciplinary action, including expulsion, and a referral to the local police department will be made if another instance occurs or if it can be shown that he has anything to do with Allison Jones becoming the subject of retaliation.

In addition, it was recommended that Raymond Hilliard be suspended for a period of three school days and be required to take the Title IX perpetrator's course. He should be sternly warned that he will be subject to further disciplinary action, including expulsion, and a referral to the local police department will be made if another instance occurs or if it can be shown that he has anything to do with Allison Jones becoming the subject of retaliation.

The final recommendation was that Allison Jones be monitored for a period of three to six months to ensure that this incident did not cause her social or academic performance to deteriorate. If there were any deterioration in either her social development or her academic performance, then the district should take the necessary steps to arrest the deterioration and place her on a plan to restore it.

The OCR rules indicate that the investigation be thorough and timely. Thorough means that everyone involved must be interviewed and all relevant information be factored into the conclusions drawn. Timely means that the investigation must begin within 24 hours of the school's getting notification and must conclude within 60 days. The rules also specify that the conclusions reached by the Title IX coordinator or investigator must be provided in writing and orally to the victim and perpetrators.

Ms. Roberta Lawrence should notify Allison and her mother that the investigation concluded with a finding that substantiated Allison's allegation. As a result of the substantiation, the perpetrator, Rodney Oldfield, will be suspended for 10 school days. Raymond Hilliard will be suspended for three days as a co-perpetrator. They will also be required to attend the perpetrator training courses as retraining. Both boys have been warned that if they or any of their friends take any action that Allison considered to be retaliatory then further disciplinary action up to expulsion for both or either boy could be taken. Allison and her mother should be advised that the school will be formally following Allison's academic progress and other aspects of Allison's development for a period of six months. Allison or her mother should be encouraged to communicate with her teachers, the school principal or the Title IX investigator if she feels the need to communicate.

The perpetrators should, according to OCR's rules, be told what their consequences are and the imperative that they take no action (and their friends should take no action) against Allison that could be interpreted as retaliation. They are to receive no information about the actions taken on behalf of Allison.

CHAPTER 8

CASE STUDY: AUTISTIC STUDENT—ELEMENTARY

What Happened

- A first grade, female, autistic student is receiving special education services as required by the Individual Disabilities Education Act.
- Student is shy and does not orally communicate very well with school staff, but her mother is able to understand her.
- Shortly after Thanksgiving break, child informs her mother that a boy is bothering her every time she goes to use the bathroom, telling her that the boy touches her on the bottom and puts his hand down her top.
- The child also tells her mother that she is afraid of this boy.
- Child's mother contacts school counselor and informs her about the allegations.
- School counselor does not provide the name and contact information for the school district's Title IX coordinator to child's mother.
- No one from the school district informs the mother of her child's Title IX rights, including, but not limited to, protection from retaliation for making the report known to the school.
- The counselor discusses the allegations with the boy.
- A few days later, after the meeting with the other student, the mother of the autistic child informs the counselor that her child says that the unwanted touching has continued and, in fact, has escalated.

- The counselor then has a meeting with the victim, the alleged perpetrator and the alleged perpetrator's father.
- The mother of the victim was not informed about this meeting.
- During the meeting, the counselor asks the victim to try to explain to the perpetrator's father what is taking place.
- The perpetrator confirms the allegations made by the victim.
- The father of the alleged perpetrator assures the counselor and the victim that he will have a discussion about this with his son.
- The perpetrator is given a five-day, out-of-school suspension.
- The perpetrator returns to school but does not receive any counseling on what is and what is not acceptable behavior.
- During winter break, the autistic child asks her older sister if she must go back to school after winter break. After the older sister tells the child that she must go back to school, the child takes out a knife and tries to kill herself.
- She is taken to the hospital, given treatment for cuts and also given antidepression medication. This is the first time that the child has required this type of medication.
- On the day before school is to start, the child asks her mother if she must go to school the next day and is told that she must do so.
- In the middle of the night, the child's mother is awakened by the screams of her daughter who is on top of her with a knife and threatening to kill her mother and then herself.
- She is taken to the hospital and stays several days in a mental health facility.
- The school is informed of what occurred during the winter break.
- School staff is informed by the mother that her daughter is afraid to return to school.
- The school does not hold an immediate individual education plan meeting but does put the child on homebound services.
- The child's IEP team meets for the first time in March, two months after the end of winter break.
- During the meeting, there is no discussion of the sexual harassment of the victim and no discussion of what, if any, impact the incidents had upon the child's ability to receive a free, appropriate, public

education. The team continues the homebound placement for the victim.

- During this meeting, the IEP team does obtain consent from the child's parents to obtain the child's hospital records.
- In April, the IEP team meets again.
- Although the child's medical records have been received, there is no discussion of the content, and the child remains on homebound status.
- While on homebound, the mother continues to take her child for mental health treatment.
- At no time was the school's Title IX coordinator involved in the investigation of the allegations made by the autistic child.
- No offer of help was made to the parents of the victim for their child.
- No notice of Title IX rights were explained to the victim's parents.
- No interim measures were offered to the victim's parents that would have enabled their child to return to school.
- Other than placement on homebound, no amendments were made to the victim's IEP.

What the School Did Correctly

Nothing.

What the School Did Wrong

Where to start? From the beginning, the school made mistakes in handling this case. When the counselor first heard of the allegations, no referral was made to a Title IX coordinator to start an investigation into the allegations. And, no one bothered to put into place interim measures to protect the victim from the perpetrator while an investigation was proceeding. Further, no one told the victim's mother of all of her Title IX rights, including the right to be free from retaliation for making the claim to school staff. No one warned the perpetrator or his parents of the consequences of retaliation.

Then, when the perpetrator continued to harass the victim, no consequences for what appeared to be retaliation were imposed upon the perpetrator. In fact, the counselor thought it was sufficient to bring the victim into a room with the perpetrator and his father to discuss what had been taking place. Somehow, the counselor thought that it was acceptable to hold this meeting without informing the victim's mother.

After winter break, and despite being informed about the two suicide attempts by the victim and a confession from the perpetrator that he did everything alleged by the victim, the school's answer was to put the victim on homebound. No relief or help was offered to the victim's mother to help her child deal with the trauma. What's more, although the victim's IEP team received medical information about the victim and all of her problems, this report was never discussed, and homebound for the balance of the school year was maintained. Out of sight, out of mind was the motto of the school district. Hence, the victim was isolated from her peers for an entire semester of school.

Consequences for the School

The mother of the victim filed a due process complaint against the school, claiming that the school denied her child FAPE when it placed her on homebound for an entire semester and in failing to discuss the situation during IEP meetings. The school district claimed that putting the victim on homebound was acceptable because it kept her away from the perpetrator and protected her from further harm. In addition, the school district claimed that the parents were making a claim under Title IX and that they could prevail only if they could prove that the school acted with reckless disregard or reckless indifference. And, because the school provided homebound the school argued, they did not act with reckless disregard or reckless indifference.

The state hearing office rejected all of the school's defenses. What's more, the hearing officer, in his ruling, was appalled by the inaction of the school staff. Accordingly, the hearing officer found in favor of the child and awarded significant compensatory educational services to the child paid for by the school to make up for all of her lost educational opportunities. After the ruling, the case was settled, and the school paid significant damages and attorney fees to the victim and her parents. In fact, two years after the ruling, in a discussion with the hearing officer in the case, he stated that he was still appalled by the inaction of the school officials and that he actually "toned down" the facts published in his written order.

How any official at the school thought what they did to respond to the allegations was acceptable is beyond belief. Sticking your head in the sand and moving the victim of sexual harassment so that no one has to deal with the problem is never, ever acceptable.

CHAPTER 9

CASE STUDY: TRANSGENDER STUDENT—HIGH SCHOOL

What Happened

- A transgender high school student goes to the school counselor's office and informs the counselor that he wants to drop out of school because he can no longer take the teasing that other students are directing towards him.
- Immediately, the counselor contacts the student's parents and the school's principal about the conversation.
- The next morning, the counselor, principal and parents meet to discuss the student's allegations.
- During the meeting, the parents inform the counselor and principal that their child has come home depressed because of the constant harassment that he is facing at school.
- After the meeting, the school does not put into place any plan to protect the student, pending its investigation of the allegations.
- Five days after the meeting, the parents come home from work and find that their child has hung himself. He leaves a note that says: "I can't take it anymore. Today the entire class teased and bullied me."

What the School Did Correctly

The counselor got the school off to a good start by first listening to the child and then immediately informing the parents of the situation. Having a meeting the next day with the parents was also good. Still, after that, not much was done to help.

What the School Failed to Do Correctly

After contacting the parents and informing them of what their son said, everything else that involved school personnel violated Title IX regulations.[23] To illustrate, at no time was the school's Title IX coordinator informed of the allegations.[24] Indeed, nothing indicated that the school had a Title IX coordinator.

Further violations of the regulations: During the meeting with the parents, no one told the parents of the Title IX rights they and their child had. Also, after the meeting, no interim measures were put into place. This fact is confirmed in the judge's ruling when he found that for five days after the meeting, the school appeared to have done nothing to help the student. In addition, at no time during the proceedings did the school submit a copy of its Title IX policies or provide the judge with any evidence that it even had Title IX policies, protocols and procedures in place that would produce a course of action after the school received a notice of a complaint of sexual harassment.

The Conclusion

The outcome of this case is undeniably tragic. Five days after the parents met with the school staff, they came home and found their child dead by suicide. As a result, the judge allowed the parents to proceed with their Title IX claim against the school and ultimately a monetary settlement was reached.

Lessons to Learn From This Case

Holding a meeting to listen to parent concerns about bullying or sexual harassment allegations directed towards their child in of itself is insufficient. In this case, the school did not appear to have in place policies, protocols and procedures that would have required the school to take immediate action to address the allegations.

No interim steps were taken that might have provided the alleged victim with some protection against the alleged perpetrators. No investigation

---

[23] *Questions and Answers on Title IX and Sexual Violence*, located at *http://www2. ed.gov/about/offices/list/ocr/docs/qa-20104-title-ix-pdf.*

[24] Assuming that the School had a Title IX Coordinator.

was started after the meeting, and no one addressed the victim's classmates to warn or remind them that if the allegations were in fact true, there would be significant consequences.

Sadly, it only took five days of inaction to produce a tragic outcome. Accordingly, school officials not only had to defend the district from litigation, they had to deal with the joint guilt and pain that many must have felt for not taking prompt action.

CHAPTER 10

CASE STUDY: STAFF PERPETRATOR—SUMMER PROGRAM

What Happened

- On July 7, 2016, the school district's superintendent received a report that a teacher was sexually molesting several students on a school bus that was transporting children between the ages of ten and twelve to and from the school-sponsored, summer activity program.

- The superintendent obtained and reviewed the security camera video on the bus for the time frame during which some of the alleged actions took place.

- At least one incident of sexual molestation by the teacher was confirmed.

- The teacher was fired, and the police were called on July 7th.

- The superintendent gave the video to the police.

- The school district has a policy that requires all staff to immediately contact the state's child abuse hotline when there is a suspicion of child abuse, including but not limited, to sexual abuse.

- The state has a mandatory reporting requirement that makes it a criminal violation if mandatory reporters, including but not limited to school employees, fail to promptly hotline a report of suspected child abuse or sexual abuse of a minor.

- No one at the school made a hotline report.

- The school district did not have a Title IX policy, and no one at the school was in charge of Title IX investigations.

- The teacher was arrested, charged with multiple criminal charges and released on bail on July 10, 2016.
- No parents of the school district were informed about the incident until Monday, August 29, 2016, when all students of the school district were given a letter to take home to their parents.
- The letter said that parents were not told of the incident prior to August 29th in order to protect their child's confidentiality.
- Several parents called the superintendent after receiving the letter, asking if their child was a victim of the perpetrator.
- The superintendent informed each parent that he could not disclose that information.
- After receiving the letter, several parents who had students attending the summer school program asked their child if anything had happened to them and some disclosed, for the first time, that the teacher had touched them in "their private areas."
- Some parents filed hotline reports of the allegations starting on August 29th.
- State employees confirmed that this was the first time that anyone in the department charged with handling hotline reports had been informed of what took place in the school on July 7th.
- A state investigation has started and some of the children have started seeing mental healthcare providers.
- Some parents have withdrawn their children from all school-sponsored, after-school activities.

Required Title 1X Compliance

If a school has in place Title IX policies, protocols and procedures, they must also be used when there are allegations of staff sexual harassment or staff sexual violence against a student.

What the School Did Correctly

Absolutely nothing.

The School District's Failures

1. The most glaring failure was not notifying parents about what happened as soon as possible.

On April 29, 2014, shortly before OCR published its lengthy document about Title IX compliance, President Obama held a press conference discussing a report that he had received from the Department of Education. That report informed the President that major colleges were not taking allegations of sexual abuse seriously and that a college had actively covered up the problem to keep it out of sight. Later that day, the OCR released its publication[25]. A component of the OCR's requirement was prompt response and to immediately put into place interim measures to help the alleged victim, including, but not limited to, an offer of counseling help to the alleged victim.

Further, parents of the alleged victim must be contacted immediately, informing them of the allegations, be given the name and contact information for the school district's Title IX coordinator and assurances that a thorough investigation of the allegations will be conducted. And if the allegations are confirmed, measures have to be put into place to help the victim feel safe at school and resources made available to help the victim with any trauma caused by the incident. In this case, none of this happened. So, victims were left to suffer for almost two months, and parents now can have no confidence that the school will act in the best interest of their children.

2. The school failed to have in place Title IX policies and did not have a Title IX coordinator.

An investigation into this case by outside authorities revealed that the school did not have in place Title IX policies, did not have a Title IX coordinator and did not have in place policies, protocols and procedures to investigate allegations of sexual harassment or sexual abuse. These are all violations of the April 2014 OCR directive.

3. The school violated state law and did not follow its own published policies regarding the reporting to state authorities when allegations of potential child abuse become known to the school staff.

---

[25] *Questions and Answers on Title IX and Sexual Violence*, located at *http://www2. ed.gov/about/offices/list/ocr/docs/qa-20104-title-ix-pdf.*

The investigation also disclosed that the school district had in place a policy that informed all staff that they were mandatory reporters of suspected child abuse. Indeed, this policy required staff to immediately use the state-provided "call hotline" to make a report when child abuse was suspected. In addition, the state had a law that requires all school staff to hotline all incidents of suspected child abuse and makes it a crime not to do so. And, if any person is punished by his or her employer for making a report, even if the allegations are found unsubstantiated, the staff person who issued the punishment also faces state criminal charges.

In this case, the school district staff failed to follow its own reporting policies and violated state laws when no hotline call report was made. And the "excuse" of confidentiality provided by the superintendent appears to be nothing more than a cover-up for the district's many failures. So, not only will the school district have to deal with investigations by government agents, but it will also have to rebuild the trust lost by many parents due to the school district's many failures, including, but not limited to, immediately informing parents of the situation.

WHAT DID HAPPEN

INTRODUCTION TO DOCUMENTED CASE STUDIES

Cases of Noncompliance from the Office of Civil Rights

Compliance is significantly complicated. In fact, it becomes an extended regimen of requirements, documentation, training, policy and procedure issues, expenses and more.

We are hoping that a review of resolution agreements signed off on by school officials after OCR found their district to be in violation of Title IX compliance requirements will give you a different look at the compliance issue. Once OCR determines that a school has violated Title IX, what the school must do to satisfy OCR can be, and often is, extensive.

Protection of students is taken very seriously by OCR and by you—we know that. We also believe, however, that protection for schools and staff is often less than it could be due to lack of compliance. Well-intentioned efforts, policies and procedures to protect students don't replace meeting the specific OCR requirements.

To that end, summaries of cases where schools were found *not to be in compliance* and the related resolution agreements follow to give you an idea of the "new normal" of compliance. Each of the schools could have avoided a long, extensive and costly problem had school officials put in the time and effort to make certain that their school's Title IX policies, protocols and procedures were up to date and in compliance with OCR Title IX regulations. And once the policies, protocols and procedures were made compliant, made certain that all staff, faithfully and without fail, followed those updated directives.

Schools have a choice: comply and protect or don't comply and suffer the consequences. Based on our experience in the field, we are not just suggesting you take the first one; we are warning you against choosing the second. Don't wait until you have a problem to update and implement compliant Title IX policies, protocols and procedures.

CHAPTER 11

SUMMARY OF MAY 13, 2016 DEAR COLLEAGUE LETTER [26]

Prior to the documented cases that follow, we felt it would be helpful to provide a summation of the May Dear Colleague Letter as a reference.

I. **Introduction**

On May 13, 2016, the Department of Justice (DOJ) and the Department of Education (DOE) published a joint Dear Colleague Letter (DCL) informing schools receiving federal funding that Title IX prohibits discrimination based upon a student's gender identity and also prohibits sexual discrimination against transgender students. In addition, the letter informs schools that this publication is to be regarded as "significant guidance" for schools receiving federal funding. Schools have been put on notice that failure to follow the requirements of the DCL will be considered in violation of Title IX, causing the loss of federal funding if the violations are not corrected. A summary of the DCL follows.

II. **The DCL Includes Definitions or "Terminology" for Purposes of Title IX**

A. **Gender Identity:** Refers to the individual's internal sense of gender. The individual's gender identity may be different or the same as the individual's sex assigned at birth.

B. **Sex assigned at birth:** The sex designation on a newborn's birth certificate.

---

[26] *Letter: Transgender Students* www.ed.gov/letters/colleague-201605-title-ix-transgender.PDF *Dear Colleague*

C. **Transgender:** Describes individuals whose gender identity is different from the sex assigned at birth. To illustrate: A *transgender male* is an individual who identifies as male but was assigned at birth as a female. A *transgender female* is an individual who identifies as female but was assigned at birth as a male.

III. Requirements for Compliance with Title IX

A. Schools must treat a student's gender identity as that student's "sex."

B. Schools cannot treat a transgender student differently from other students of the same gender identity.

C. When a student or the student's parent or guardian notifies a school that his or her child will identify with a specific gender identity then, from that point forward, the school must interact and treat that child consistent with his or her gender identity.

D. A school cannot require the child or the child's parent or guardian to provide a medical diagnosis or seek "treatment" before treating the student consistent with his or her requested gender identity.

E. Even if other students, parents or community members object to treating a transgender student consistent with the student's gender identity, the school must comply with the requirements of Title IX.

    1. The DOJ and DOE point out that the desire to accommodate others' discomfort will not justify an illegal policy and has never been recognized as an excuse for noncompliance with other civil rights antidiscrimination laws.

F. Harassment based upon gender identity, transgender status or gender transition is harassment based upon sex.

    1. If this occurs, the school **must take prompt and effective steps** to end the harassment, prevent recurrence and remedy its effects.

G. Schools must treat students consistent with their gender identity, even when the student's educational records or identification documents indicate a different sex.

1. Schools must identify the student using the pronoun and name consistent with the student's gender identity.

H. A school's failure to treat students consistent with their gender identity may create or contribute to a hostile environment and is a violation of Title IX.

I. In addition, all of the Title IX guidelines contained in OCR's April 29, 2014 publication, Questions and Answers on Title IX and Sexual Violence, apply to transgender students.

IV. **Sex-Segregated Activities and Facilities**

A. Transgender students must be allowed access to restrooms and locker rooms consistent with their gender identity. Title IX is not violated if a school offers all of its students individual user options strictly on a volunteer basis. When a school offers single-sex classes, a student must be allowed to attend the class that is consistent with his/her gender identity.

B. Schools may operate or sponsor sex-segregated athletic teams when selection for the teams is based upon competitive skills **or** when the activity involved is a contact sport.

1. Title IX does not prohibit age-appropriate, tailored requirements based upon what the DCL calls "sound, current and research-based medical knowledge," regarding the impact of the student's participation on the competitive fairness or physical safety of the sport.

2. Yet, the DCL provides no guidance as to what is and what is not "sound, current and research-based medical knowledge."

C. Although Title IX does permit schools to provide separate housing on the basis of sex, they must allow the transgender student access to the housing consistent with the student's gender identity. This rule also applies when schools need overnight accommodations on field trips. If the school requires students to share rooms on overnight field trips, transgender students must be allowed to stay in a room consistent with their gender identity.

D. D. Schools may not punish a student for dressing in a manner consistent with his or her gender identity nor can schools exclude a student from participating in a school-sponsored activity consistent with his or her gender identity or that does not conform to what the DCL refers to as "consistent with stereotypical notions of masculinity or femininity."

V. Privacy and Education Records

A. The DCL says that protecting transgender students' privacy is critical. This will help ensure that these students will be treated consistent with their gender identity.

B. If a school fails to take reasonable steps to protect students' privacy related to their transgender status, this will be a violation of Title IX.

C. Schools may maintain records of the student's sex assigned at birth or birth certificate but must keep these records confidential. Disclosure without prior authorization or unless permitted under a FERPA (Family Educational Rights and Privacy Act) exception will be considered a violation of Title IX.

D. Title IX requires schools to respond to a request to amend information about a student's transgender status consistent with a school's practices in handling requests to amend records from other students. If schools treat the request from a transgender student differently from requests made by students who are not transgender, this is a violation of Title IX.

E. If a transgender student or his or her parent or guardian complains about how the request for the amendment of the student's records has been handled by the school, **the complaint must be promptly and equitably resolved under the school's Title IX grievance procedure.**

   1. So, in these cases, not only must the complaint procedures of FERPA be followed but also the mandates of Title IX.

   2. This adds another item to the list of things that the school's Title IX coordinator must address.

Conclusion: What Happens Now

The administrative branch of the federal government has left no doubt that transgender students are entitled to Title IX protection and that gender identity harassment constitutes illegal discrimination. That said, there is already pushback against what some consider an abuse of power by the DOJ, DOE and OCR, and some governors have announced their refusal to comply. Last year, two members of the Senate held hearings condemning what they considered an abuse of power by OCR when that agency announced its rules against bullying. It would not be a surprise, therefore, for this DCL to come before a Senate committee to discuss what authority the DOJ and the DOE had to issue this document.

Still, one Circuit Court, the Fourth in *G.G. v. Gloucester County School Board,* 116 LRP 15374 (4th Cir. April 19, 2016), has endorsed the directive published in the DCL. And, if schools elect not to comply, unless stopped by a federal court or Congress, there will be threats of loss of federal funding. Until the Supreme Court or Congress rules otherwise, the best practice for schools would be to take steps to comply with the DCL.

CHAPTER 12

FAILURE TO ADDRESS ALLEGATIONS OF HOSTILE SEXUAL ENVIRONMENT

Minot State University in North Dakota was found to be in violation of Title IX by the Office for Civil Rights. On July 7, 2016, Minot State University entered into a resolution agreement with the Office for Civil Rights after an investigation by OCR determined that the college had violated Title IX.

The following violations were found by OCR:

- Failure to promptly respond to student allegations that a hostile environment existed at the college.
- Failure to coordinate allegations of sexual assault with the college's own law enforcement personnel. In fact, OCR found that out of four allegations of sexual assault made to campus police, Minot conducted only one Title IX investigation.
- Minot's Title IX policies and procedures did not comply with Title IX.
- Minot's notice of nondiscrimination did not comply with Title IX.

Accordingly, Minot agreed to the following corrections within the resolution agreement that it entered into with OCR and what can gleaned from them follows:

Minot had to:

- Offer students who were the victims of sexual harassment or assault, at the college's expense, counseling and other appropriate remedies to address emotional, psychological, academic or employment issues faced by the victim caused by Minot's delay in processing Title IX complaints. The expense of paying for counseling, in of itself, should motivate all schools to become compliant with the OCR's Title IX requirements.

- Develop a procedure to document each incident or complaint of discrimination on the basis of sex received by the college. Use of a software program would be a more efficient response to this requirement versus attempting to use a manual, uncentralized method of tracking data.

- Submit for OCR's review and approval, copies of all grievances filed with the college and related to investigative documentation during the 2015-2016, 2016-2017 and 2017-2018 academic years that allege sexual assault and sexual harassment. They are now subject to micromanaging by OCR.

- Hire an equity consultant with expertise in all areas of compliance with Title IX. This is another name for hiring a qualified Title IX coordinator.

- Conduct periodic climate checks to assess the effectiveness of steps Minot has taken to provide everyone a campus free of sexual assault and harassment. This can only be done by data collection. Again, a software program would be the most efficient method for collecting and then reviewing collected data.

In addition, Minot must:

- Revise its Title IX policies, grievance procedures and code of conduct, including its notice of nondiscrimination and grievance procedures to make certain that the revised versions provide for prompt and equitable resolution of complaints of sexual harassment or sexual assault.

- Develop a written protocol between its police and Minot's Title IX coordinator that requires prompt notification of each other about complaints of sexual assault and sexual harassment and also provides how both will work together coordinating the investigation of these complaints.

- Periodically review the terms of its memorandum of understanding with the Minot Police Department to improve communications and coordination regarding allegations of sexual assault and sexual harassment.
- Provide training to students and staff on its revised Title IX policies and grievance procedures.
- Create a committee to identify strategies for ensuring that students understand their Title IX rights.

Conclusion

Not only did Minot incur expenses from the failure to comply with Title IX, the failure will consume staff time that could have been better spent on educating students instead of keeping OCR staff updated on compliance matters. *This case serves as a warning to all schools that receive federal funding of how expensive it can be to ignore allegations of sexual assault or sexual harassment.* To illustrate, OCR has taken the position that it has the power to order violating schools to pay for counseling needed by victims of sexual assault and sexual harassment and hire more staff to make certain that no future violations of Title IX occur. And once OCR finds violations, they stay around to look for more violations. Also, OCR involvement is only the start of problems for the offending school. Next will come lawsuits asking for damages and attorney fees. Even if the school prevails in those cases, the cost for legal expenses in defending against these claims would far exceed the cost to implement Title IX compliant policies, protocols and procedures. Become Title IX compliant before OCR comes calling.

CHAPTER 13

FAILURE TO PROTECT RIGHTS OF THE ACCUSED

Wesley College, Dover Delaware, was found in violation of Title IX by the Office for Civil Rights. On October 12, 2016, OCR found that Wesley College violated Title IX because it did not properly protect the rights of students accused of sexual harassment of other students.

The violations found by OCR were:

- Failure to interview the accused students during the investigations into the complaints.
- Failure to allow the accused student the opportunity to fully respond to the charges and rebut the allegations of sexual harassment made against the accused.

In addition, the OCR found that Wesley College also violated Title IX in the following areas:

- Interim measures, such as counseling and adjustments to the academic schedule of the alleged victim, were not offered.
- Too little time was spent by Wesley to conduct valid investigations into complaints, preventing Wesley from gathering all pertinent evidence.
- Failure to notify all parties of the outcome of investigations of the complaints.

- Failure to provide a notice of nondiscrimination informing students and staff of the name of the individual at the college who would investigate and resolve all Title IX complaints.
- Failure to adopt Title IX policies and procedures that identified time frames for all stages of the Title IX grievance process and the name of all deputy Title IX coordinators.

Each of the above violations is not uncommon. Indeed, all could have been avoided if the Wesley staff had taken time to review the requirements published by the Office for Civil Rights on April 29, 2014.[27]

Accordingly, Wesley entered into a resolution agreement with OCR that required Wesley to do the following:

- Publish an anti-harassment statement.
- Revise the college's Title IX grievance procedures.
- Publish the new Title IX policies and procedures.
- Provide Title IX training to all Wesley employees immediately and thereafter on a regular basis. Provide Title IX training to all Wesley students immediately and thereafter on a regular basis.
- Reinvestigate all allegations of sexual harassment from 2013 through 2015, and correct all deficiencies that OCR found during this investigation by OCR.
- Convene a Title IX committee, composed of staff and students, to develop a plan for educating Wesley employees and students about sexual harassment and sexual violence.
- Provide OCR with copies of all reported incidents of alleged sexual harassment and sexual violence to Wesley for the 2016-2017, 2017-2018 and 2018-2019 academic years.

Conclusion

Failure to protect the accused revealed how delinquent Wesley College was in handling sexual harassment and sexual violence complaints. The lesson to be learned is that a failure to review and then follow the "suggestions" published by the Office for Civil Rights in April of 2014 will produce significant and expensive consequences for the offending

---

[27] *Questions and Answers on Title IX and Sexual Violence*, located at *http://www2. ed.gov/about/offices/list/ocr/docs/qa-20104-title-ix-pdf.*

school. Now Wesley will be subjected to strict scrutiny by the OCR at least through the middle of 2019. Failure to review and then address a school's current Title IX policies, protocols and procedures to be certain that they are in compliance will result in significant scrutiny by an agency of the federal government and cost that school more than it would have spent to prevent the problem from ever arising.

CHAPTER 14

SEXUAL HARASSMENT OF STUDENT BY SCHOOL STAFF MEMBER

Included in Title IX Prohibitions

Failure to investigate a student's allegation of sexual harassment by one of the Hunter College's professors was found to be a violation of Title IX by the Office for Civil Rights.

Title IX not only prohibits peer-on-peer sexual harassment and sexual violence but also prohibits staff-on-student sexual harassment or sexual violence. And failure to take immediate steps to investigate allegations of sexual harassment of staff against a student will result in a finding of a Title IX violation by the OCR.

During its investigation, the Office for Civil Rights made the following conclusions:

- The college failed to take prompt and equitable action to investigate the allegations.
- The college failed to assess the need and provide for interim measures to protect the alleged victims during its investigation of the complaint.

The need to provide interim measures to protect the alleged victim(s) from the alleged perpetrator after a complaint of sexual harassment or sexual violence has been made is a critical early piece in ensuring that prompt and equitable action is taken by a school once notice of an allegation is received. Making certain that an alleged victim feels safe while attending classes is a must first step. That said, prompt resolution of the allegation is vital because if the allegations are found to be unsubstantiated, any interim steps taken against the alleged perpetrator that may have interfered with that person's access to the educational environment must quickly end.

In the Hunter situation, the college failed to:

- Assess whether or not a hostile environment existed on its campus.
- Adopt and publish grievance procedures that complied with the requirements of Title IX.
- Publish notice of its policy of nondiscrimination.
- Provide students and staff the name of and contact information for its Title IX coordinator.[28]

Accordingly, Hunter College entered into a resolution agreement with OCR, requiring the college to do the following:

- Rewrite its Title IX grievance procedures to make certain they complied with the Title IX procedures outlined by OCR.[29]
- Train all staff on the requirements of Title IX compliance.
- Provide annual training to all students about Title IX policies and procedures, including discussion of the anticipated revisions to the college's Title IX grievance procedures.

And that wasn't all—during its investigation, OCR found that the school mishandled 12 Title IX complaints filed during the 2011-2012 and 2012-2013 academic years. The college now must address those concerns, which will include providing remedies for those students who were the victims in those cases.

Hunter also had to review all complaints filed during the 2013-2014, 2014-2015 and 2015-2016 academic years to determine whether or not those complaints were handled in compliance with Title IX. And, for those cases that were not handled properly, the college had to provide

---

[28] *Questions and Answers on Title IX and Sexual Violence*, located at *http://www2. ed.gov/about/offices/list/ocr/docs/qa-20104-title-ix-pdf*. Indeed, the last three bullet points are requirements contained within this Department of Education Document.

[29] *Questions and Answers on Title IX and Sexual Violence*, located at *http://www2. ed.gov/about/offices/list/ocr/docs/qa-20104-title-ix-pdf*

the victims appropriate relief including, but not limited to, counseling paid for by the college, academic relief and, when needed, reimbursement for tuition.

Having to go back five years for any school would be difficult. And because OCR will have oversight, if the federal agency is not satisfied with the relief proposed in any or all of the cases to be reviewed, the college will need to offer additional relief, all at no cost to any of the students who were harmed. The failure to comply with Title IX when sexual harassment or sexual violence complaints are lodged against staff can also be costly and the requirements time-consuming.

CHAPTER 15

TITLE IX AND TRANSGENDER STUDENTS

Introduction

Transgender students' right to use the bathroom and locker room consistent with their gender identity has been the subject of intense debate. The answer to the debate, however, might be close at hand as the United States Supreme Court has elected to hear the complaint of a transgender student claiming that his Title IX rights were violated when his school denied him the right to use the bathroom and locker room consistent with his gender identity.[30] If the Supreme Court continues to have eight judges when it rules, there are three possible impacts of the Court's order.

If a majority uphold the ruling of the Court of Appeals for the Fourth Circuit,[31] then the "law of the land" would make it a violation of Title IX for any school receiving federal funding to prevent a transgender student from using the bathroom and locker-room consistent with the student's gender identity.

If the majority reverses the ruling of the Court of Appeals for the Fourth Circuit, then Title IX is not violated if a school denies transgender students the right to use the bathroom consistent with their gender identity and would be a reversal of the Department of Education's directive that

---

[30] *G.G. v. Gloucester County School Board*, 116 LRP 45595 (*Cert. Granted*, S.Ct. October 28, 2016)

[31] *G.G. v. Gloucester County School Board*, 116 LRP 15374 (4th Cir. April 19, 2016)

schools must allow transgender students the right to use the bathroom and locker room consistent with their gender identity.[32]

If the final vote is four to four, then the Fourth Circuit ruling remains in effect, but the law is only binding for Maryland, Virginia, West Virginia, South Carolina and North Carolina.

The Office for Civil Rights' Position

If the Supreme Court upholds the Fourth Circuit Court ruling[33], then the Department of Education's Office for Civil Rights directive issued on June 21, 2016 to the Dorchester County School District Two in South Carolina is an example of how OCR will deal with schools that do not permit transgender students to use bathrooms and locker rooms consistent with their gender identity.[34] In this case, OCR found that the District's Title IX policies and procedures did comply with Title IX. The OCR did, however, find that the district violated Title IX when it denied a female transgender student the right to use the girls' bathroom. Accordingly, the district entered into a resolution agreement with OCR. The district was required to:

- Allow the student to use the girls' bathroom.
- Make certain that the student's access to all school activities was based upon her gender identity.
- Revise its Title IX policies and procedures to include a prohibition against gender-based discrimination.
- Provide periodic training to school and district level administrators on the district's obligation to prevent and address gender-based discrimination.

Conclusion

If the Supreme Court reverses the Fourth Circuit, then no school will be obligated, under Title IX, to allow students to use the bathroom or locker room consistent with their gender identity. If the Supreme Court is evenly

---

[32] http://www2.ed.gov/about/offices/lost/ocr/docs/faqs-title-ix-single-sex-201412.pdf.

[33] G.G. v. Gloucester County School Board, 116 LRP 15374 (4th Cir. April 19, 2016)

[34] Dorchester County (SC) School District Two, 116 LRP 26974 (Office for Civil Rights Southern Division, D.C. (South Carolina, June 21, 2016)

divided, then this South Carolina district would still need to follow the terms of the resolution agreement because all South Carolina schools that receive federal funding are within the jurisdiction of the Fourth Circuit. There is a need for all schools that receive federal funding to monitor the outcome of the pending case before the Supreme Court and act accordingly once the Court's ruling is made public.

Note: We have provided a summary of the DCL regarding transgender in the appendix for you.

APPENDIX

POLICIES, PROCEDURES AND MORE

INTRODUCTION

Following this introduction, you will find an extensive compliance kit, a summary of model policies and sample victim and perpetrator letters— all of which you are free to use and/or modify to fit your needs. For informational purposes, we have included a journal article by one of the authors, Larry Altman, JD.

Many school districts are aware that they have unanswered obligations to Title IX and state laws that require an extensive and organized data system to eliminate bullying. Most, if not all, administrators, teachers, counselors and school nurses recognize the need to structure an effort to prevent everything from bullying to sexual violence within their schools— issues that cause physical and emotional issues for the victims, including the tragedy of suicide.

Some are just hoping that the regulations will go away and, until that happens, they can stay under the radar because coming into compliance and doing what is needed will be difficult. The Office for Civil Rights (OCR) has gone on record as stating that they are now turning their attention from universities to school districts. Friends, the rules and regulations aren't going to go away. Just like Title VII for employers, in the future, the regulations will probably expand, rather then contract. We, at IntegraEd, have a solution to recommend.

IntegraEd provides a comprehensive Title IX solution that will bring your school district into full compliance with the prevention aspects of the regulations, provide the guidance you need for incident examination and tracking, as well as provide a host of additional services, including an application that can be loaded on a student's smartphone, focusing

111

on suicide prevention and the ability for students to report bullying in real time.

So, what are the consequences of being out of compliance?

- Your failure to comply becomes a part of the public record—-meaning a bad reputation for the school, you and its school board.
- Your school risks its Title IX funding.
- Your school gets to endure years of OCR close scrutiny and condemnation.
- Perish the thought that there is a suicide or death in your school related to bullying, but the reality is that it happens. While we are all working to prevent this, if it does happen in your school, know that some smart plaintiff's lawyer will easily figure out if you were out of Title IX compliance. You, your school board members, the faculty and staff involved will all get to endure the civil suit.
- This situation could likely be a job or career killer. You may have been working hard to prevent bullying and its repercussions, but if you are out of compliance, you are out of compliance— discussion over. We strongly encourage you to add comprehensive compliance to your other efforts to protect students.

We also understand that the Title IX mandates are onerous. To be in compliance, every school district that accepts Title IX funds must do the following:

- Designate and provide extensive and specific training for a Title IX coordinator.
- Provide extensive and specific training for every faculty and staff member, *including vendors and substitute teachers.*
- Provide extensive and specific training for every student in age-appropriate language. This essentially means providing a specific course for college students, for middle and high school students and for elementary school students. This training must be translated into different languages, depending on the English competency of the international student. Additionally, this training

must include a testing element to determine comprehension on the part of the student.

- Provide specific rehabilitative training for perpetrators of sexual violence and sexual harassment.
- Develop an extensive set of definitions, policies and protocols relating to the prevention of Title IX violations.
- Develop a comprehensive set of forms and procedures relating to conducting investigations of Title IX complaints.
- Develop and implement a comprehensive set of remedies for victims and perpetrators once investigations have been completed. The objective is to prevent incidents from recurring and to mitigate the effects of discrimination and eventually eliminate bullying in the school.
- Develop and take specific steps to prevent suicide in the school.
- Collect "big data" to review and analyze the organizational trends relative to sexual violence in the school district.

We get that no individual school district can possibly come into full compliance on its own. That is the reason IntegraEd is your best option for discipline issues.

We provide a software method to keep track and aggregate data *relative to all discipline matters* within your school district. They can be bullying incidents, IDEA /mental health worries, 504 matters, run-of-the-mill discipline matters and/or virtually any incident you need to keep in school records.

We provide a turn-key, fully comprehensive Title IX solution.

- The Title IX coordinator's course (without a testing component).
- The all-faculty and staff course (with a testing component).
- A training program for college students (with a testing component).
- A training program for middle and high school students (with a testing component).
- A training program for third through sixth grade students (with a testing component).
- A training program for K through second grade students (without a testing component).

- A training program for those found to be perpetrators (of sexual violence) at the elementary school level.
- A training program for those found to be perpetrators (of sexual violence) at the middle school and high school level.

We also provide:

- The required proactive training, the definitions, forms and protocols assuring—once adopted and implemented—that your school district is in compliance with all Title IX obligations.
- The forms and protocols to address the reactive steps you need to take once you are notified of an allegation of sexual harassment or sexual violence.
- The technology for tracking and documenting your compliance.
- Access to technology support—*on a 24/7 basis.*
- Seven days per week telephone support on an unlimited basis for your Title IX coordinator, so, if needed, he or she can call an IntegraEd professional and get one-on-one guidance as incidents are reported.
- Quarterly updates as OCR mandates change. Our lawyer will note those changes, and we will pass them on to you, so you don't have to wonder if you are continuously up to date.

Additional Optional Services:

- A therapist on staff, who can provide contracted counseling for traumatized students as needed.
- Contracted Title IX investigations of allegations of sexual violence.
- A contracted Title IX coordinator to handle all the Title IX issues for your school district.
- The Organizational Climate Study, which OCR will require when you have a Title IX complaint.

By taking advantage of IntegraEd's services, you will be protected against the scrutiny of OCR and, in the event of a lawsuit, be in a far stronger position legally. It is a win all the way around—your students will be protected, your school district (and board) will be protected and so will you (professionally).

INTEGRAED COMPLIANCE KIT

The district superintendent or university chancellor should formally adopt the following:

IntegraEd Suggested Title IX Organizational Structure

The new regulations require each school district to declare or assign a Title IX coordinator and IntegraEd has advised you of the requirements the regulations specify for that position previously in the book. We recommend that each district or university adopt the following organizational structure. Please feel free to put your school or university name on any of the information, definitions, statements, policies and/or procedures that follow and use them as your own.

Each district shall establish a response team made up of at least two teachers (depending on the size of the district or university, select a greater number), at least two nurses and at least two school counselors. A minimum of two is required in each category, so if one is not available, the other probably will be when the need to activate the response team arises. These professionals will be the ones to assist the Title IX coordinator to conduct investigations and, perhaps more importantly, work with the victim to take the interim measures necessary to assure that the protections that are required get implemented.

Additionally, at each school there should be a Title IX liaison identified. This person is accountable to the district Title IX coordinator. The Title IX liaison makes sure that the teachers in his/her school upload the school roster data, expose all students to the various training programs and is the person to whom that teacher, staff, students and others report any incidents of Title IX. The Title IX liaison notifies the Title IX coordinator of an alleged incident and the response team is notified that an investigation at that school is required.

We encourage you to take any of the following and call it your own. Know that the school included—district, college, university—is arbitrary, as they are interchangeable and can also be adjusted to fit not only your school, but your specific needs. The entire process looks like this:

Proactive Steps:

- District Title IX coordinator is named and advertised throughout the district.
- A district Title IX response team is identified and members are oriented to their roles.
- A Title IX liaison at each school is named and oriented to his/her role.
- The principal at each school notifies all of his/her students, parents, faculty and staff of the existence and role of the school's Title IX liaison.
- The Title IX liaison makes sure that each and every faculty, staff, and student (in his/her school) takes his/her respective training course and records/captures data.

At this point, the school district is in compliance with the Title IX expectations.

Immediate Reactive Steps:

- A faculty member or staff member gets notified that there has been an incident of sexual harassment or violence by a student. At this point, new obligations (and liability) are present.
- The person who was notified of the alleged incident now has to notify the school's Title IX liaison of the incident.
- The liaison notifies the district's Title IX coordinator and the district response team regarding the alleged incident.
- Title IX coordinator activates the response team and schedules the investigation.
- Investigation begins and the interim measures to protect the alleged victim are taken.

Follow-Up Steps:

- The investigation proceeds (must start within 24 hours of notice and conclude no later than within 60 days).
- Interim protective steps are taken by response team.
- The investigation concludes, either substantiating the allegation or not.
- Conclusions are made and appropriate follow-up action is taken.
- Notification of findings is published.

Definition of Sexual Violence

Physical sexual acts perpetrated against a person's will or where a person is unable to give consent because of the person's age, intellectual disability or due to the use of drugs or alcohol.

Definition of Sexual Harassment

Sexual harassment is discrimination based upon gender identity or failure to conform to stereotypical notions of masculinity or femininity. Same-sex conduct may give rise to a claim of sexual harassment.

Definition of a Hostile Sexual Environment and When a Situation Becomes One

A hostile sexual environment exists when, "conduct of a sexual nature is sufficiently severe, persistent or pervasive so as to limit a student's ability to participate in or benefit from the education program, or to create a hostile or abusive environment." This cannot be "banter" but, rather, persistent or pervasive misconduct that has the effect of limiting the student's ability to participate in or benefit from the educational program offered by the school.

When determining whether or not a hostile sexual environment exists, schools must determine whether or not the misconduct rose to the level of denying a student educational benefits from the educational program.

Statement of the School's Title IX Jurisdiction

The XYZ School District or University (insert formal name of your school or university) formally acknowledges that it has the jurisdiction to and the formal obligation to implement the rules and regulations specified in Title IX.

Statement Prohibiting Discrimination

It is the policy of The XYZ School District or University (insert formal name of your school or university) to prohibit discrimination on the basis of sex or sexuality on our campus or in any setting relating to our school activities. Education has become heavily governed by a number of federal and state statutes: Title IX of the Office for Civil Rights, the Individual Disability Education Act and Section 504 of the Rehabilitation Act. It is our policy to prohibit discrimination under these and other related acts.

Statement Prohibiting Retaliation

It is the policy of XYZ School District or University (insert formal name of your school or university) to prohibit retaliation in any form directed at an alleged or affirmed victim of sexual harassment or sexual violence. Our district (or university) will inform all alleged victims of sexual violence that Title IX includes protection against retaliation. We will take all reasonable steps to prevent retaliation from occurring. We will take prompt, strong action against anyone who attempts to retaliate against an alleged victim of sexual violence or sexual harassment or a person reporting an act of sexual violence or sexual harassment.

Policy for How Long to Collect Data on Victim's Performance

It is the policy of XYZ School District or University (insert formal name of your school or university) to monitor the performance of any victim of sexual harassment or sexual violence for a minimum of six months past the point of the determination made by our Title IX coordinator that discrimination has occurred. Our Title IX coordinator will monitor the various aspects of the student's performance and behavior, noting if there is a drop-off or diminishment in his/her performance or behavior from that noted prior to the incident of discrimination. If such a drop-off or diminishment is noted at any time during the six-month monitoring period, then the appropriate personnel will be assembled and modifications to the student's individual education plan (IEP) will be made. All efforts will be made to assist the student in his/her recovery.

Policy for Sanctioning Perpetrators

It is the policy of XYZ School District or University (insert formal name of your school or university) to provide sanctions for perpetrators. If an individual is found by the Title IX coordinator to have discriminated against another student, our policy is to impose appropriate disciplinary action up to and including expulsion from the district (or university), potentially moving the perpetrator to another school, potentially moving the perpetrator to other classes within the same school and requiring the perpetrator to attend mandatory rehabilitation training. It is our policy that the perpetrator understands that what he/she did was not acceptable conduct.

Policy for Notification of Outcome of Investigation

It is the policy of XYZ School District or University (insert formal name of your school or university) to notify in writing the parties to a formal investigation of Title IX related sexual harassment or sexual violence of the outcome or findings of the investigation within 10 days of the conclusion of the formal investigation. Our district (or university) will notify all formal parties (excluding witnesses) to the investigation of the outcome or findings of the investigation. The victim will be advised of the outcome and will also be advised regarding the remedies specified, including what steps we will take to protect the victim from further discrimination or retaliation. The perpetrator will only be informed of the sanctions to be taken against him/her, not the protections or steps to be taken relative to the victim.

Policy on How We Respond to Victims

It is the policy of XYZ School District or University (insert formal name of your school or university) to respond to victims of sexual harassment or sexual violence with compassion and culturally competent counseling. Our district (or university) will consult with local gay-straight alliances and other student-initiated groups to help advise the Title IX coordinator, the Title IX liaison and the members of the school-specified response team as to how to effectively address Title IX mandates. Additionally, we will provide appropriate interim measures to alleged victims including:

- Providing an escort so that the alleged victim does not have to navigate the building alone where he/she could again become a victim or become subject to retaliation.
- Moving the alleged victim so that he/she does not have to have contact with the alleged perpetrator.
- Modifying the class schedule or timetables for completion of school requirements.
- Providing counseling, tutoring or other measures necessary to mitigate the effects of the discrimination.

Policy on Confidentiality

It is the policy of XYZ School District or University (insert formal name of your school or university) that only the Title IX coordinator can make the decision to honor an alleged victim's or a bystander's request for confidentiality. We understand the student's interest in maintaining his/her confidentiality relative to reporting incidents of sexual harassment or sexual violence. The faculty or staff person who receives the initial notification from an alleged victim or potential bystander shall advise the student that he/she has the option to request confidentiality and about the availability of confidential advocacy, counseling and other support services, as well as the right to file a Title IX complaint with the school and to report a crime to campus police or local law enforcement. Additionally, the faculty or staff person who receives the initial complaint must advise the complainant that he/she has the obligation to report the incident to the Title IX coordinator.

Policy on Disciplinary Code and Consequences for Violating Code

It is the policy of XYZ School District or University (insert formal name of your school or university) that the district (or university) has a disciplinary code that says if an individual is found by the Title IX coordinator to have discriminated against another student, our policy is to impose appropriate disciplinary action up to and including:

- Expulsion from the district (or university).

- Potentially moving the perpetrator to another school.
- Potentially moving the perpetrator to other classes within the same school.
- Excluding the perpetrator from extracurricular school activities.
- Requiring the perpetrator to attend mandatory rehabilitation training.

Policy Relating to International Students Who Become Victims

It is the policy of XYZ School District or University (insert formal name of your school or university) that the district (or university) to afford Title IX protections to international students, regardless of their immigration status, including undocumented, who become victims of sexual harassment or sexual violence. We recognize that unique issues arise for these individuals, and we will allow them to drop below the mandatory full-time caseload if necessary. We will provide documents and training in the language that the international student, who is an English language learner, understands. We will also take steps to prevent recurrence of any sexual harassment or sexual violence, and we will take steps to remedy the discriminatory effects on the complainant and other students.

Designation of Reasonable Time Frames

It is the policy of XYZ School District or University (insert formal name of your school or university) that the district (or university) begins the planning and preparation steps for the investigation of the Title IX complaint within 24 hours of the initial notice provided by an alleged victim or from a bystander. The actual investigation shall commence within 72 hours of notice provided. The investigation shall be completed within a 60-day period from the actual commencement of the investigation, and formal findings or conclusions will be provided in writing to the required parties within 10 days of the conclusion of the investigation.

Procedures for Reporting a Title IX Complaint

It is the policy of XYZ School District or University (insert formal name of your school or university) that the district (or university) will provide training for all our district's (or university's) faculty, staff and students regarding the requirements of and our obligations to Title IX. Included in that training will be the procedures for reporting a complaint. Additionally, the reporting procedures will be contained herein. Each school will designate a Title IX liaison. Every employee in every school from the custodian to the principal will be prepared via training to receive a Title IX complaint. That district (or university) personnel will notify the Title IX liaison who will start the process to initiate the investigation and also start the process to consider the appropriate interim measures to protect the alleged victim. The Title IX liaison will notify the Title IX coordinator, who will notify the Title IX response team (made up of at a minimum two teachers, two nurses and two counselors).

Procedures for Conducting Investigations

It is the policy of XYZ School District or University (insert formal name of your school or university) that the district (or university) will conduct a thorough investigation of any and all Title IX complaints. The procedure will be as follows:

First:

The Title IX coordinator or his/her designee will receive the initial information from the Title IX liaison. The next step is to conduct a private interview with the alleged victim or the bystander who initially reported the incident. If this individual is a minor, his/her parent or guardian will be notified and asked to be present. The interviewer will advise the alleged victim of his/her various rights under Title IX and assure that those rights will be protected. This includes the notion that the Title IX investigation can proceed simultaneously with any investigation from law enforcement. The interviewer will collect the who, what, when, where and why in as exacting detail as is possible, given the age and intellectual capacity of the interviewee. Additionally, the interviewer will collect the names of any and all witnesses named and also begin to determine the interim measures needed to provide protection to the student. These interim measures will be discussed with the response team and then implemented immediately.

Second:

The alleged perpetrator will be interviewed. If this student is a minor, then his/her parent or guardian will be invited to be present. He/she will be advised of his/her rights and the requirement for confidentially as this is a formal investigation. He/she will be advised regarding the allegation or allegations against him/her and asked to confirm or deny the allegation or allegations. The alleged perpetrator's account will be collected, and the interviewer will collect the names of any and all witness named. The alleged perpetrator should be advised to take no steps or any action regarding retaliation against the alleged victim or bystanders and to instruct others that the advice regarding retaliation applies to them as well. This point must be emphasized that if it does happen (if retaliation is deemed to be present), then much harsher sanctions will be imposed.

Third:

All witnesses specified by the alleged victim and the alleged perpetrator will be interviewed. They will be advised of the need for confidentiality, as all parties have rights. They should be advised not to make the alleged incident and this interview the subject of gossip or loose talk, as it is so important. They should be asked for their insight into what happened as they observed or overheard and should be advised that the interviewer is interested in facts and their feelings. In addition, they should be asked what they know to be true and if they think the alleged perpetrator has it in his/her character to do what has been alleged to have occurred. They should be asked if the alleged victim and the alleged perpetrator has credibility (in the witness' eyes). These points are particularly important, as few incidents are actually "black or white." The Title IX requirements are that if a preponderance of the findings (evidence) is 50.1% or more that the perpetrator did commit the discrimination, then the benefit of the doubt shall be given to the victim. These feelings of the witnesses can contribute greatly to the findings or outcome of the investigation. The investigator can also solicit information or insights from others, including faculty or staff who are in a position to provide relevant information or insights because they know both or all parties. They may not have insights into the facts of the incident, but they can contribute insights in the character of the alleged victim, alleged perpetrator and the witness interviewed. A determination of the credibility of the victim and/or the perpetrator is helpful here.

Fourth:

The investigator may return to the alleged victim or the alleged perpetrator after the witness interviews to clarify any additional information that surfaced from the witness interviews. Once all the information is collected, the Title IX coordinator, the Title IX liaison (for that school) and the response team should meet to review the findings. The Title IX coordinator makes the final determination to substantiate the allegation (to find it factual) or to overturn the allegation (to find it a fiction) or to find that there was not enough information to make a determination. Remember the requirement regarding preponderance of the findings (evidence) that if it is 50.1% or more, then the perpetrator committed the discrimination, and the benefit of the doubt shall be given to the victim. The investigation should be completed within 60 days from the initial notice point.

Fifth:

The findings shall be conveyed in writing to the relevant parties within 10 days of the conclusion of the investigation. The sanctions to be imposed if the perpetrator is found responsible shall be implemented. The remedies to the victim shall be implemented.

Sixth:

The 180 days monitoring of the victim will determine if there is a need to continue to monitor or the need exists to modify the individual education plan of the victim.

Seventh:

The Title IX coordinator will articulate the steps that will be taken to prevent a reoccurrence of any sexual harassment and or sexual violence and, as appropriate, remedy the discriminatory effect on the complainant and other students.

Philosophy and Strategies for Bystanders to Intervene

We at (insert formal name of your school or university) want to create an educational setting that is safe. We are mandated by Title IX to protect all students from sexual harassment and sexual violence. We include the special needs of international students, transgender students and students covered under the IDEA and Section 504. We are committed to the elimination of retaliation directed at alleged victims and whistle blowers (bystanders). Having said all of the above, we encourage all students that "if they see something, to say something." We encourage all bystanders to engage in the process of protecting their fellow students. If instances occur where some students are not accepted or appreciated— if they are being abused, discriminated against or mistreated, they, under Title IX, must be protected and the school and university officials need all eyes helping. If a student feels comfortable or confident enough to actually step in to stop the discrimination or abuse, then they will be supported by administration for doing so. Alternatively, effort to report the incident is just as acceptable. In an evolved setting like our school, we work daily toward the reduction and eventual elimination of sexual harassment and sexual violence. The school should be a zone free of this abuse and discrimination. In reality, there aren't enough adults to make this happen. In reality, it will take the active participation of bystanders becoming Good Samaritans to facilitate the shift to full acceptance of all students.

Definition of Consent (for older students)

It is the policy of XYZ School District or University (insert formal name of your school or university) that if the student is under the age designated by our state (to give consent) due to the presence of a intellectual disability or due to the presence of drugs or alcohol, then consent (to sexual contact) cannot be present.

OCR requires that all school districts and universities articulate and publish their grievance procedure. IntegraEd recommends the following to be in compliance:

Detailed Grievance Procedure

1) Adopt the provided statement of the school's jurisdiction over Title IX complaints.
2) Adopt and include the provided definitions of sexual harassment and sexual violence.

3) Adopt and include the provided explanation of when sexual harassment and sexual violence create a hostile sexual environment.

4) Adopt the reporting policies and protocols provided.

5) Adopt the provisions for confidential reporting and the granting of confidentiality provided.

6) Adopt the provisions/policies for prohibiting retaliation provided.

7) Include the notice to the alleged victim that the Title IX investigation can occur simultaneously to a criminal complaint and an investigation by law enforcement.

8) Adopt the provided provisions for providing notice for interim measures to provide protection to the complainant.

9) Adopt the provided provisions that the evidentiary standard that the school must take in determining whether or not the allegations are true shall be by a preponderance of the evidence (50.1% or greater) means that the evidence must show that more likely than not the perpetrator committed the act of sexual harassment or sexual violence.

10) Adoption of the provided notice of potential remedies for the victim.

11) Adoption of the provided notice of the potential sanctions that can be taken against the perpetrator, which include disciplinary action up to expulsion from the district or university; being moved to a different school within the district; having the schedule and class assignment changed; removal from school activities and the requirement for rehabilitation training.

12) Notice to victims regarding local sources of counseling, advocacy and support.

13) Notice to students, parents (of elementary and secondary students) faculty and staff regarding who the Title IX coordinator and who the individual school's Title IX liaison are and their contact information, so they will know to whom they can report complaints and will know the grievance procedures.

14) Notice to students and parents of elementary and secondary students regarding how the school's grievance procedures apply to complaints filed by students or complaints filed on their behalf.

15) Adopt the provided provisions for adequate, reliable and impartial investigations of complaints, including the provision that witness on both sides will be included and considered.
16) Adopt the provided time frames for completion of the major stages of the complaint process.
17) Adopt the provided notices to the complainant and alleged perpetrator of the outcome of the complaint.
18) Adopt the provided policy that the school or university will, in writing, take steps to assure that it will take steps to prevent recurrence of any sexual harassment and sexual violence and, as appropriate, will remedy the discriminatory effects on the complainant and other students.

DISTRICT VIOLENCE REPORT FORM

Note: This form is to be maintained by the Title IX liaison designated for each school.

When a staff, faculty member, student or a student's parent advises any district or university personnel of a Title IX complaint, that employee shall immediately report the incident to the designated Title IX liaison.

The Title IX liaison shall complete this form and then transmit the information immediately to the Title IX coordinator.

1. _____(student) from_____ (school) made the initial report or contact (with the district or university) personnel.

Date and time_____

2. _____Employee who received the initial report.

Date and time_____

3. Date and time report was made to the Title IX liaison_____

4. What was reported to have happened and to whom and by whom?

_____

_____

_____

_____

_____

_____.

If additional space is needed, then use an additional page.

5. Were any witnesses identified?

_____

_____

6. What additional information was collected or assessed as important?

_____

_____

7. Date and time Title IX coordinator notified_____

Signed _____

    Title IX Liaison   Date and time_____

HIGHLIGHTS OF DEPARTMENT OF EDUCATION'S MAY 13, 2016 PUBLICATION EXAMPLES OF POLICIES AND EMERGING PRACTICES FOR SUPPORTING TRANSGENDER STUDENTS[35]

Introduction

In addition to the joint publication issued on May 13, 2016 by the DOJ and DOE,[36] the DOE also published this document in the form of a Q and A. What follows, therefore, is a brief summary of some of the highlights.

Within schools' antidiscrimination policies, it must state that sex discrimination includes discrimination based upon gender identity and expression.

In order to provide support to transgender students, schools should communicate, to all students, that resources are available to help transgender students who may experience mental health disorders such as depression, anxiety and posttraumatic stress. In addition, the school should inform transgender students that the school has staff who are competent to provide support and services to any student who has questions related to transgender identity.

Interpretation

This document presumes that the school has psychologists, school counselors, school nurses or social workers, who have the expertise to

---

[35] Department of Education May 13, 2016: www.ed.gov/oese/oshs/emerging practices.PDF

[36] *Dear Colleague Letter: Transgender Students* www.ed.gov/letters/colleague-201605-title-ix-transgender.PDF

assist these students. **This assumption presumes a lot, and more likely than not schools do not have in-house people with this knowledge.**

In OCR's April 29, 2014 publication, Questions and Answers on Title IX and Sexual Violence, Section B-2, OCR says that schools have the Title IX responsibility to be certain that school counselors and others responsible for receiving and responding to Title IX complaints receive "appropriate training about working with LGBT and gender-nonconforming students **and** same-sex sexual violence." Further, in Section J-3, OCR informs schools that school staff involved in implementing the school's grievance procedures must have training or have the requisite knowledge of the effects of trauma including neurobiological changes *and* cultural awareness training regarding how sexual violence or sexual harassment impacts students differently because of their cultural background. OCR is informing schools that they must have available experts who know and understand the mental health issues that transgender students may have so that when these students seek help, there is a competent person available. A failure to have these available experts would be a violation of Title IX.

SAMPLE LETTER TO VICTIM'S PARENTS/GUARDIANS

(date)

(name of parents or guardians)

Re: Outcome of Investigation of Sexual Harassment

Dear (name) :

I am writing to inform you that (school or district) has completed its investigation into the complaint that (name of victim) was sexually harassed by one of her (or his) peers. After a thorough investigation that included interviews with (name of victim), (school) staff and the perpetrator, we concluded that (name of victim) was sexually harassed.

Accordingly, (name of principal), principal of (name of school), met with the perpetrator, disciplined the student in accordance with the (name of school) (name of school's policy), and warned the perpetrator that a repeat of this misconduct against (name of victim) or any other student would result in additional and harsher discipline.

School staff will closely monitor (name of victim) performance at school because if we believe that due to this incident, some services need to be added to assist (name of victim) with her (or his) education and feeling safe at school, we would contact you to discuss our suggestions. Further, if you notice any negative changes at home that are impacting (name of victim), please immediately contact staff at (name of school) so that they can meet with you to discuss what might be done at school to help her (or him) get past any difficulties that might arise because of this incident.

If (name of victim) or you learn that the perpetrator or friends or relatives of the perpetrator have done anything directed at (name of victim) that might be deemed as retaliation for the filing of her (or his) complaint, please let the principal of (name of school) know immediately. Title IX protects victims of sexual harassment and sexual assault from any form of retaliation. (name of school) staff takes retaliation seriously and will promptly investigate allegations of retaliation. And, if retaliation occurs, prompt and harsh action will be taken against (name of school) students who participated in the retaliation. As a result, although the Title IX investigation process has been completed, (name of school) will continue to closely monitor (name of victim) and her (or his) school performance so that she (or he) continues to receive a free and appropriate public education.

If you do not agree with this determination, you may appeal to (name of district superintendent) by submitting a letter of appeal within five workdays of the date of this letter to (name and address of chief legal counsel).

On behalf of (name of school), we regret that the incident took place. If you have any questions, do not hesitate to contact me.

(Title IX coordinator's name and choice of closing.)

SAMPLE LETTER TO PERPETRATOR'S PARENTS/GUARDIANS

(name of parents or guardians)

Re: Outcome of Complaint of Alleged Sexual Harassment

Dear (name):

I am writing to inform you that (school) has completed its investigation into a complaint that your student (name), sexually harassed or sexually assaulted one of his (or her) peers. After a thorough investigation that included interviews with the victim, (name of school) staff, another child who was accused of participating in the harassment or assault and your child, we concluded that (name) did participate in the sexual harassment or assault of a student.

Accordingly, (name), principal (or administrator) of (school) met with you and (name) to discuss the incident, disciplined (name) in accordance with the (name of school) Student Code of Conduct and warned your student that a repeat of this misconduct against the victim or any other student would result in additional and harsher discipline.

Further, (student) needs to understand that he (or she) cannot do anything directed at the victim that we may conclude to be retaliation for filing this claim with (school) staff. In fact, if (name) encourages others to retaliate against the victim for filing this claim, it will be treated as if he (she) committed the act of retaliation. Title IX protects victims of sexual harassment and sexual assault from any form of retaliation.

(school) staff takes retaliation seriously and will promptly investigate allegations of retaliation. And, if retaliation occurs, prompt and harsh action will be taken against (school) students or staff who participated in the retaliation. As a result, although the Title IX investigation process has been completed, (school) will continue to closely monitor the situation.

If you do not agree with this determination, you may appeal to (name of district superintendent or school administrator) by submitting a letter of appeal within five (5) workdays of the date of this letter to: (name and address of chief legal counsel).

If you have any questions, do not hesitate to contact me.

(Title IX coordinator's name and choice of closing.)

FAIR WARNING:
STUDENT MENTAL HEALTH ISSUES AND THE LAW

By: Lawrence J. Altman[37]

It's common knowledge that children and adolescents face emotional challenges, at home and at school, as they travel through the stages of growth from child to young adult. Fitting in, peer pressure and changes in their physical make-up, both brain and body, are, for the most part, expected. But what about children who fight more than the "normal" emotions, those who have been determined to have a mental illness? A study by The Child Mind Institute concluded that out of a population of 74.5 million children, 17.1 million would have a diagnosable mental illness with serious impairments before they are eighteen years old.[38] What's more, the *Journal of Adolescent Health* published a study finding that transgender teenagers faced a higher risk of being diagnosed with a

---

[37] Lawrence J. Altman is an adjunct professor at Avila University in Kansas City. Until his retirement in 2016, Mr. Altman was the Special Education and Section 504 Lead Attorney and Compliance officer for Kansas City Public Schools, as well as the Title IX Coordinator for the district. Mr. Altman graduated in 1976 from St. Louis University Law School and currently is the chairperson of the Missouri Bar's Joint Task Force on Lawyers Helping Lawyers and the co-chair of the Missouri Bar's Lawyers' Assistance Committee.
[38] Merikangas,K., Hep,J.,Burstein, M., Swanson,S.,Avenevol, S., Cui, L., Benejet, C., Swendsen, J. (2010). *Lifetime Prevalence of Mental Disorders in U.S. Adolescents:* Results from the National Comorbidity Survey Replication—Adolescent Supplement (NCS-A). Journal of American Academy of Child and Adolescent Psychiatry.49(10): 980-989. doi:10.1016/j.jaac.2010.05.017

mental illness when compared to non-transgender teenagers. [39] Examples of the laws regulating schools with regard to diagnosed and suspected mental health issues abound. In November of 2014, the Connecticut Office of the Child Advocate concluded that because the school district failed to consider Adam Lanza's mental health problem, this may have been a contributing factor in the horrific outcome of Sandy Hook.[40] In *Estate of Barnwell by Barnwell v, Watson*[41], the court denied the school's motion to dismiss the parents' Title IX and Section 504 claims that the school's failure to address their child's mental health problems was a contributing factor to the child's death by suicide.

Students with mental health issues are protected by federal and state laws that school administrators and their attorneys must know and address. What follows, therefore, is a review of legal obligations imposed upon schools for students who have or are suspected of having mental health issues.

I. Section 504 of the Rehabilitation Act

Through a 2012 Dear Colleague Letter from the Office of Civil Rights, schools were made aware of an expanded interpretation, and therefore compliance with, of the disability qualifications of Section 504 of the Rehabilitation Act of 1973, as established by Congress when it enacted the *ADA Amendments Act of 2008.*[42] The letter included the Section 504 definition of disability: "(1) a physical or mental impairment that substantially limits a major life activity." OCR said that this broader definition of the ADAAA's disability qualifications would no longer

---

[39] Sari L. Reisner, Sc.D. M.A., Ralph Vetters, M.D. M.P.H., M. Leclerc, M.P.H., Shane Zaslow, M.A. M.S., Sarah Wolfrum, M.P.H., Daniel Shumer, M.D., and Matthew J. Mimiaga, Sc.D., M.P.H. *Mental Health Transgender Youth in Care at an Adolescent Urban Community Health Center: A Matched Retrospective Cohort Study,* Journal of Adolescent Health xxx (2015) 1-6

[40] Sarah Healy Egan, Faith VosWinkel, Julian D. Ford, Christopher Lyddy, Harold Schwartz, Andrea Spencer, *Shooting at Sandy Hook Elementary School,* THE CONNECTICUT OFFICE OF THE CHILD ADVOCATE (November 21, 2014) available at http://www.ct.gov/oca/lib/oca/sandyhook11212014.pdf.

[41] 44 F. Supp. 3d 859 (E.D. Ark. 2014)

[42] Americans with Disabilities Act Amendments Act of 2008, 42 USCA § 12101, Public Law 110-235, ADAAA

require extensive analysis by the school staff, nor could mitigating factors, like medications, be used to determine a child's 504 qualification. If a school concludes that a student, who has a confirmed diagnosis of PTSD, bipolar disorder or major depressive disorder, *does not* have a qualifying 504 disability, OCR will demand that the school provide substantial evidence to support this conclusion. Accordingly, although OCR says that no psychological condition will always qualify a student under 504, it has put schools on notice that at least three diagnosed mental health conditions will, with very limited exceptions, qualify a child as having a Section 504 disability.

And 504 disabilities are not limited to those that impact learning. OCR has stated: "Therefore, rather than considering only how an impairment affects a student's ability to learn, a recipient or public entity must consider how an impairment affects any major life activity of the student and, if necessary, assess what is needed to ensure that the student has an equal opportunity to participate in the recipient's or public entity's program."[43] Accordingly, if a student has a mental health issue that substantially limits the child's ability to have an equal opportunity to participate is a public school's activities, that child has a 504 disability.

Further, parents need not produce medical documents in order for their child to be assessed or to qualify for a 504 disability. In fact, schools have an affirmative duty to locate, assess and, for those who have a Section 504 disability, provide the child with reasonable accommodations.[44] So, when the school determines a student has a mental health issue that rises to the level of a 504 disability, the next step to be taken is to determine what, if any, reasonable accommodations must be put into place by the school that would allow the student to have equal access to the educational services, academic and nonacademic, offered to all students.

For students who present with mental health issues, however, this may create challenges for the schools, unless someone employed by the school is trained to recognize symptoms of mental illness and, once that

---

[43] *Dear Colleague Letter,* 58 IDELR 79 (Office for Civil Rights, January 19, 2012) available at http://www2.ed.gov/about/offices/list/ocr/letters/colleague-201109.html.
[44] *Pine Forest (AZ) Charter School* 116 LRP 19095 (Office for Civil Rights, Western Division, Denver (Colorado) 08-15-1293, March 17, 2016)

has been determined, help school staff put reasonable accommodations into place. Some schools may now have an obligation to obtain and pay for outside expert services so that the OCR's 504 mandates can be met.

II. Title IX

The Office for Civil Rights, on April 29, 2014, informed schools receiving federal funding that Title IX contains a mental health component that must be addressed.[45] OCR requires schools to provide counseling to victims of sexual assault, sexual violence and sexual harassment. Schools are also required to have an on-call expert in providing trauma-informed services to victims of sexual violence or sexual harassment. In addition, if the victim of sexual violence or sexual harassment is an IDEA or Section 504 student, the school must determine whether or not the child would require additional services, including, but not limited to, psychological or counseling services, so that the child can continue to receive a free appropriate public education. If the perpetrator is an IDEA or 504 student, the school must also determine whether or not the student is in need of psychological or counseling services to not only prevent recurrence but to also make certain that the child continues to receive FAPE. Because the IDEA[46] and Section 504[47] both contain a "child find" requirement, the April 29th publication places an affirmative obligation upon schools to assess victims of sexual violence or sexual harassment who, prior to the incident, were not disabled under the IDEA or 504, yet may have developed a qualifying disability under either law. According to OCR, therefore, Title IX contains a mental health component that schools must properly address for victims and perpetrators of sexual violence and sexual harassment.

OCR is not alone in making this a requirement. For example, in *Estate of Barnwell by Barnwell v, Watson*[48], parents of a student who died by suicide filed a Title IX and Section 504 claim against the school district. Their Title IX claim alleged that the school failed to take steps to curtail

---

[45] *Questions and Answers on Title IX and Sexual Violence*, located at *http://www2. ed.gov/about/offices/list/ocr/docs/qa-20104-title-ix-pdf.*

[46] 34 CFR 300.111

[47] 34 CFR 104.35

[48] 44 F. Supp. 3d 859 (E.D. Ark. 2014)

sexual harassment against their child, knew that this was causing their child significant mental health issues, yet took no steps to assist their child. The parents, moreover, alleged that the school's failure to act, including failure to account for the mental harm done to their child, caused their child to commit suicide. The judge denied the school's motions to dismiss the Title IX claim, holding that in the five days between being informed of the alleged acts of sexual harassment and when the child died by suicide, the school failed to take any action. The judge concluded that the school's failure to take any action, if proven at trial, would result in a finding that the school violated the Title IX rights of the child and entitle the parents to a judgment in their favor.

Transgender Students

On May 13, 2016, the Department of Justice and the Department of Education published a joint Dear Colleague Letter informing schools receiving federal funding that Title IX prohibits discrimination based upon a student's gender identity and prohibits sexual discrimination against transgender students.[49] In addition, all of the Title IX guidelines contained in OCR's April 29, 2014 publication, *Questions and Answers on Title IX and Sexual Violence* [50] applies to transgender students. The April 2014 publication said that school staff involved in implementing the school's grievance procedures must have training or have the requisite knowledge on the effects of trauma, including neurobiological changes *and* cultural awareness training, regarding how sexual violence or sexual harassment impacts students differently because of their cultural background.

In addition to this joint publication with the DOJ, the DOE published a document titled *Examples of Policies and Emerging Practices for Supporting Transgender Students*[51] The DOE informed schools that in order to provide support to transgender students, schools should communicate to all students that resources are available to help transgender students who

---

[49] Dear Colleague *Letter: Transgender Students* www.ed.gov/letters/colleague-201605-title-ix-transgender.PDF

[50] *Questions and Answers on Title IX and Sexual Violence,* located at *http://www2. ed.gov/about/offices/list/ocr/docs/qa-20104-title-ix-pdf.*

[51] Department of Education May 13, 2016: www.ed.gov/oese/oshs/emerging practices.PDF

may experience mental health disorders such as depression, anxiety and posttraumatic stress. The school should also inform transgender students that the school has staff that is competent to provide support and services to any student who has questions related to transgender identity. A failure to have these available experts would be a violation of Title IX.

III. Individuals With Disabilities Education Act

IDEA recognizes that some students may have a mental health issue that rises to the level of a qualifying IDEA disability. Federal regulations define emotional disturbance as:

"A condition exhibiting one or more of the following over a long period of time *and* to a marked degree that adversely affects a child's performance:

A. An inability to build or maintain satisfactory interpersonal relationships with peers and teachers.

B. Inappropriate types of behaviors or feelings under normal circumstances.

C. A general pervasive mood of unhappiness or depression.

D. A tendency to develop physical symptoms of fears associated with personal or school problems."[52]

The Office of Special Education Programs reminded schools that the IDEA requires schools to assess a child's needs in all areas of suspected disabilities including, but not limited to, the child's emotional status. [53] If the assessment shows that the child has an emotional disturbance, as defined by federal regulations, then the child has an IDEA disability.

That said, some IDEA students may start to exhibit mental health issues not seen before the development of the child's existing individual educational plan. In those cases, if the school fails to account for what may be a new problem and the failure to respond causes the child to be denied a FAPE, consequences for the failure to act could occur.

---

[52] 34 CFR 300.8 (c)(4)(i)

[53] *Dear Colleague Letter,*115 LRP 33911 (Office of Special Education Programs, July 6, 2015)

To illustrate, in *District of Columbia Public Schools*,[54] the hearing officer ruled that the school district denied a student with an IEP a free appropriate public education when the school failed to amend the student's IEP after learning that the child had anxiety and severe depression that caused the child to frequently miss school. In this case, the child was a high school student, who was hospitalized three times during the school year due to self-mutilation and suicidal ideation. During the IEP meetings, parents and school staff discussed the student's mental health problems that caused significant absences from school. Yet the school failed to make significant changes to the student's individual education. Citing *Kevin T. v. Elmhurst Comm. Sch. Dist. No.205*[55] and federal regulations[56] as authority, the hearing officer ruled that the school district denied FAPE to the student when it failed to revise the student's IEP to include a strategy to address the student's attendance problems caused by the mental health issues. As a result, the school had to provide compensatory educational[57] services to the student that included counseling at no cost to the family.

Closer to home, a Missouri due process hearing officer found that a school violated the IDEA and denied a child a FAPE when it failed to convene the child's IEP team after receiving information that the child, for the first time, had been hospitalized after attempting suicide and threatening the mother's life. The hearing officer ruled that once the school was put on notice that the student had been hospitalized due to a significant mental health problem, IDEA required that the school immediately convene the child's IEP team to review the existing educational plan and determine whether or not modifications to the plan would be needed so that the child would continue to receive a FAPE. And, failing to have the meeting to discuss any new needs for the child violated the IDEA.[58] What this points to is that some states hearing officers, around the country, have found schools in violation of the IDEA when the school failed to address

---

[54] 116 LRP 7639 (SEA DC December 22, 2015)

[55] *Kevin T. Elmhurst Com. Sch. Dist. No. 205,* 36 IDELR 153 (N.D. Ill.2002)

[56] 34 CFR Sect. 300.324 (b)(1)(ii)

[57] 116 LRP 7639 (SEA DC December 22, 2015)

[58] *St. Louis City School District,* 114 LRP 35586, 12 ECLPR 11, (#14-0250 ED, August 4, 2014)

a significant mental health care problem for a student receiving IDEA services.

IV. Missouri Enacts Student Suicide Prevention Statute

On June 4, 2016, Gov. Nixon signed into law House Bill 1583 that included a statute requiring all Missouri public schools to have a policy in place for youth suicide and prevention by July 1, 2018.[59] The policy must include staff training on strategies for identifying students who may be at risk for suicide, how to assist a student who may be at risk for suicide and protocols for responding to a student suicide death. The bill also requires the Missouri Department of Elementary and Secondary Education to develop and publish a model policy that complies with the statute no later than July 1, 2017. Starting July 1, 2018, Missouri law has added a mental health component for schools to address.

V. Conclusion

Three federal laws—IDEA, Section 504 of the Rehabilitation Act and Title IX—have a mental health component that public schools must consider when presented with a student with mental health issues. In addition, starting July 1, 2018, Missouri public schools must have in place policies, protocols and procedures that will train all staff on how to react when there are concerns that a student may be at risk for suicide and how to respond when the risk is confirmed. Indeed, this is a requirement to respond when a student presents with a potentially significant mental health issue.

Failure to comply with any of the federal laws can result in school liability. To illustrate, when a school has failed to review an IDEA student's individual education plan, state hearing officers have ruled this to be a violation of the IDEA. In two of these cases, schools were ordered to provide to the student, at no cost, compensatory educational services.[60] Also, a federal judge in Arkansas refused to dismiss a Title IX and Section 504 claim filed against a district when a student died by suicide five days after the school was informed that the disabled student may

---

[59] Section 170.048 Missouri Revised Statutes
[60] *District of Columbia Public Schools*, 116 LRP 7639 (SEA DC December 22, 2015), *St. Louis City School District*, 114 LRP 35586, 12 ECLPR 11, (#14-0250 ED, August 4, 2014)

have been the victim of illegal bullying and sexual harassment.[61] In addition, the Department of Education and the Office for Civil Rights have promulgated publications notifying schools that receive federal funding that Section 504 imposes upon schools an obligation to provide to disabled students that have significant mental health issues reasonable accommodations that may include counseling services.[62] And the DOE and OCR have informed schools receiving federal funding that victims of sexual violence or sexual harassment may require schools to provide these victims counseling when the incidents cause the victims to manifest significant mental health issues.[63]

Schools that fail to review the impact that severe mental health issues may have upon a student risk significant consequences.[64] Schools should be proactive and not reactive when put on notice that a student suffers from significant mental health issues. Accordingly, best practice, so that schools comply with federal and state laws, is to promptly review the impact that a significant mental health illness of a student has upon the student's ability to receive a free, appropriate, public education and, when a negative impact is found, take immediate and effective steps to make certain that the student continues to receive a FAPE.

---

[61] *Estate of Barnwell by Barnwell v, Watson*, 44 F. Supp. 3d 859 (E.D. Ark 2014)

[62] *Dear Colleague Letter*, 58 IDELR 79 (Office for Civil Rights, January 19, 2012) available at http://www2.ed.gov/about/offices/list/ocr/letters/colleague-201109.html.

[63] *Questions and Answers on Title IX and Sexual Violence*, located at http://www2. ed.gov/about/offices/list/ocr/docs/qa-20104-title-ix-pdf.

[64] *District of Columbia Public Schools*, 116 LRP 7639 (SEA DC December 22, 2015), *St. Louis City School District*, 114 LRP 35586, 12 ECLPR 11, (#14-0250 ED, August 4, 2014)

Dr. Steve Cohen is the president of the Labor Management Advisory Group, Inc., a human resources management consulting firm, as well as the president of HR Solutions On-Call, a service which provides anytime access to expert advice related to safeguarding businesses and solving management issues.

With 35 years of experience in the field of human resource management, Dr. Cohen is a well-known, national authority for his expertise in resolving management "messes" from infrastructure to compliance and avoiding litigation. He has worked with staffs from two to 17,000, deftly implementing management changes and, in many cases, serving as a temporary human resource officer while handling complicated issues or assisting in the search for new management personnel.

His in-depth knowledge of today's regulatory environment and the laws impacting businesses and organizations is extensive. Dr. Cohen also applies outstanding communication and negotiation skills to create "win-win" outcomes for both businesses and employees in seemingly impossible situations.

Dr. Cohen has a MA in Public Administration from Central Michigan University, an Ed.D in Educational Psychology from Northern Illinois University and certification in Alternative Dispute Resolution from DePaul University, School of Law. He combines his knowledge of human nature with the logistics of business management for his highly successful approach to business management.

In addition, Dr. Cohen is sought after for his management and motivational training programs, helping to turn businesses into high performing organizations. He has extended his outreach to the business world with his entertaining and informative books: Mess Management: Lessons From a Corporate Hit Man and Ministry Mess Management.

Lawrence J. Altman is an adjunct professor at Avila University in Kansas City, Missouri. Until he retired in January of 2016, Mr. Altman was the Special Education Lead Attorney and Compliance Officer for Kansas City Public Schools and the Title IX Coordinator for the Kansas City School District. Prior to that position, he was a practicing attorney in St. Louis County for 34 years. In addition to membership in the Missouri Bar, he is a member of the Kansas City Bar Association and the National School Board Association's Counsel of School Attorneys.

Two of Mr. Altman's areas of focus throughout his career have been assistance for children with special needs who qualified for services under the federal Individuals with Disabilities Act and those needing accommodations under Section 504. In 2015, the National School Board Association appointed him to serve on the in-house school counsel committee of the Council of School Attorneys Association. He was honored by the Annie Malone Children and Family Service Center in St. Louis as one of their Advocates of the Year.

Children and clients are not the only ones to benefit from his services. He has worked to help others as an active mentor in the Missouri Lawyers Assistance Program, where he was awarded the Warren Welliver Award for his efforts, compassion and concern regarding the emotional and mental health needs of those in the profession. In 2014, Mr. Altman was appointed by the Missouri Bar to serve as chairperson for its Joint Task Force on Lawyers Helping Lawyers and as the co-chair of the Missouri Lawyers' Assistance program. In 2015, the American Bar Association appointed him to serve on the Commission on Lawyer Assistance Program's Senior Lawyer Committee.

With over 35 presentations and 13 published articles regarding legal issues to his credit, Mr. Altman continues to write and present on current topics, including assistance and compliance with Title IX and other federal and state laws affecting educational venues. He currently serves on the

DESE Legislative Workgroup for the Prevention of Student Bullying and Suicide, as chair for the group developing model policies to prevent student bullying.

Printed in the United States
By Bookmasters

Printed in the United States
By Bookmasters